READING AND WRITING IN PRESCHOOL

Best Practices in Action
Linda B. Gambrell and Lesley Mandel Morrow,
Series Editors

Connecting research findings to daily classroom practice is a key component of successful teaching—and any teacher can accomplish it, if he or she has the right tools. The Best Practices in Action series focuses on what elementary and middle grade teachers need to do "on Monday morning" to plan and implement high-quality literacy instruction and assess student learning. Books in the series are practical, accessible, and firmly grounded in research. Each title provides ready-to-use lesson ideas, engaging classroom vignettes, discussion questions and engagement activities ideal for professional learning communities, and reproducible materials that purchasers can download and print.

Teaching Informational Text in K–3 Classrooms:
Best Practices to Help Children Read, Write, and Learn
from Nonfiction
Mariam Jean Dreher and Sharon Benge Kletzien

Reading and Writing in Preschool:
Teaching the Essentials
Renée M. Casbergue and Dorothy S. Strickland

Oral Language and Comprehension in Preschool:
Teaching the Essentials
*Lesley Mandel Morrow, Kathleen A. Roskos,
and Linda B. Gambrell*

Literacy Learning Clubs in Grades 4-8:
Engaging Students across the Disciplines
Heather Kenyon Casey

Breaking Through the Language Arts Block:
Organizing and Managing the Exemplary Literacy Day
Lesley Mandel Morrow, Kenneth Kunz, and Maureen Hall

Reading and Writing in Preschool

Teaching the Essentials

Renée M. Casbergue
Dorothy S. Strickland

Series Editors' Note by
Linda B. Gambrell and Lesley Mandel Morrow

THE GUILFORD PRESS
New York   London

Library of Congress Cataloging-in-Publication Data

Casbergue, Renée Michelet, author.
   Reading and writing in preschool : teaching the essentials / Renée M. Casbergue,
Dorothy S. Strickland.
      pages cm.—(Best practices in action)
   Includes bibliographical references and index.
   ISBN 978-1-4625-2347-4 (pbk. : acid-free paper)—ISBN 978-1-4625-2348-1 (hardcover
: acid-free paper)
   1. Language arts (Preschool)   I. Strickland, Dorothy S., author.   II. Title.
   LB1140.5.L3.C37 2016
   372.6—dc23
                                                            2015016849

To Daniel Casbergue and Emily Casbergue Forrester
—my first early literacy teachers
—R. M. C.

To all those who work enthusiastically and tirelessly
to help young children grow and learn
—D. S. S.

About the Authors

Renée M. Casbergue, PhD, is the Vira Franklin and James R. Eagle Professor of Education at Louisiana State University, where she is Director of the Early Childhood Education teacher preparation program and is a member of the literacy faculty. A former classroom teacher and reading specialist, she has served as president of the Literacy Development in Young Children Special Interest Group of the International Reading Association (IRA; now the International Literacy Association). Dr. Casbergue received a grant from the U.S. Department of Education's Early Reading First (ERF) program to create centers of excellence for early literacy in preschool classrooms in New Orleans public schools after serving as a consultant and external evaluator for ERF projects in four other states. She has published widely on effective learning and teaching in preschool and the primary grades.

Dorothy S. Strickland, PhD, is the Samuel DeWitt Proctor Professor of Education (Emerita) at Rutgers, The State University of New Jersey, and Distinguished Research Fellow of the National Institute for Early Education Research. A former classroom teacher, reading consultant, and learning disabilities specialist, she is a past president of both the IRA and the Reading Hall of Fame. Dr. Strickland is a recipient of the Outstanding Teacher Educator of Reading Award from the IRA, the Outstanding Educator in the Language Arts Award from the National Council of Teachers of English, and the Ferguson Award for Outstanding Contributions to Early Childhood Education from National Louis University. She has published numerous articles, book chapters, and books on early childhood education.

Series Editors' Note

A great deal of attention must focus on literacy development in early childhood. We know that young children have literacy skills, even though the literacy they demonstrate is not conventional. Emergent literacy behaviors have implications for instructional practice and later reading success. Like a child's first words and first steps, learning to read and write should be exciting and rewarding.

Currently there is a great deal of discussion about the importance of universal preschool in our country. Research demonstrates the powerful effects that preschool has on a child's readiness for kindergarten and later literacy development. We also know that access to preschool is particularly important for children who are vulnerable. At a time when policymakers are beginning to notice the crucial role of preschool literacy development, it is essential to have good resources for educating and guiding preschool teachers that reinforce the following beliefs:

1. Teachers must be aware that children come to school with unique and varying degrees of prior knowledge about reading and writing and build on that knowledge.
2. Literacy learning requires a supportive positive school environment rich with accessible materials and varied experiences.
3. Teachers must serve as models for literacy behavior by scaffolding and demonstrating strategies to be learned.
4. During their literacy experiences, children should interact within a social context to share information and learn from one another.
5. Early reading and writing experiences are motivating when they are relevant and concrete; these activities should actively engage children.

6. Early reading and writing experiences need to provide systematic and explicit skill instruction.
7. A literacy development program should focus on experiences that integrate reading, writing, listening, speaking, and viewing within the language arts and in content areas such as music, art, social studies, science, and play.
8. Diversity in cultural and language backgrounds must be acknowledged and addressed in early literacy development.
9. Differences in literacy development will vary and are addressed with small-group and one-to-one differentiated instruction.
10. Assessment of achievement should be frequent and match instruction, and multiple formats for evaluating a student's literacy development should be used.
11. Standards for early literacy benchmarks should be tied to instruction and used as a means for reaching goals for all children to read fluently by the end of third grade.
12. Instruction must be age-appropriate for the development of children, with high and achievable expectations.

Literacy development must focus on both learning and teaching. Teachers must explicitly instruct children while also encouraging them to be actively involved in experiences where they can explore, experiment, and collaborate with others. Children must be motivated to view reading as a relevant act and to associate it with pleasure.

Reading and Writing in Preschool: Teaching the Essentials addresses the essential research-based areas of reading and writing development that are linked to early literacy success—especially children's concepts of print, phonological awareness, and alphabetic knowledge. An important emphasis in this book is that reading and writing entail not only decoding of words, but comprehension of what is read, listened to, and written. The authors, Renée M. Casbergue and Dorothy S. Strickland, do an impressive job of balancing attention to print and meaning, and they confront some of the pervasive myths about preschool literacy.

While the authors focus on the importance of helping children to develop foundational concepts about reading and writing, they never lose sight of the central notion that learning does not happen in the absence of interesting things for children to read and write about. This book is filled with examples of how teachers can bring literacy learning to life in the classroom and home environments, including shared reading and writing, name games, class journals, and the use of digital technology.

You will find a wealth of knowledge and ideas for teaching the essentials of reading and writing in preschool as the authors describe the journey children embark on as they become increasingly independent readers and writers. The chapters on assessing reading (Chapter 6) and writing (Chapter 7) are particularly insightful, with practical suggestions for assessing children's progress. Casbergue and Strickland contend that teachers need to conduct meaningful assessments to help identify children who might need intensive support as well as those who might need enrichment beyond the general curriculum.

Reading and Writing in Preschool is filled with actual classroom examples of ideas and techniques that will empower teachers with the tools needed to guide young children's literacy development. We all want our students to become engaged and enthusiastic literacy learners. This book will serve as a rich and valuable resource for teaching the essentials of reading and writing in preschool.

This book is designed to complement and be used with another book, *Oral Language and Comprehension in Preschool: Teaching the Essentials*, by Lesley Mandel Morrow, Kathleen A. Roskos, and Linda B. Gambrell. Both of these preschool books in our Best Practices in Action series draw on research, theory, policy, and practices that have proved successful in developing literacy. Both books take into account the joint position statement of the International Literacy Association (ILA) and the National Association for the Education of Young Children titled *Learning to Read and Write: Developmentally Appropriate Practices for Young Children* (1998), as well as the ILA's position statement *Literacy Development in the Preschool Years* (2006). They also consider the National Reading Panel Report (National Institute of Child Health and Human Development, 2000), the National Early Literacy Panel Report (National Center for Family Literacy, 2004), and the Common Core State Standards (National Governors Association Center for Best Practices & Council of Chief State School Officers, 2010).

Children come to school with diverse social, emotional, physical, and intellectual abilities and achievement levels. They have diverse cultural backgrounds, experiences, and exposures to literacy. Teachers must know how to address all of these factors. The preschool books in our Best Practices in Action series embrace a comprehensive perspective toward literacy instruction by selecting the best techniques based on sound learning theories, such as a constructivist model or a problem-solving approach to more explicit instruction.

LINDA B. GAMBRELL, PhD
LESLEY MANDEL MORROW, PhD

REFERENCES

International Literacy Association. (2006). *Literacy development in the preschool years*. Newark, DE: Author.

International Literacy Association & National Association for the Education of Young Children. (1998). *Learning to read and write: Developmentally appropriate practices for young children.* Washington, DC: Authors.

National Center for Family Literacy. (2004). *National Early Literacy Panel report.* Louisville, KY: Author.

National Governors Association Center for Best Practices & Council of Chief State School Officers. (2010). *Common core state standards.* Washington, DC: Authors.

National Institute of Child Health and Human Development. (2000). *National Reading Panel report: Teaching children to read.* Washington, DC: Author.

Preface

Literacy matters—even in preschool. Maybe *especially* in preschool. Early childhood educators have long maintained that the seeds for lifelong learning and development are sowed before children begin formal schooling. In the now distant past, preschool programs were mostly concerned with encouraging social, emotional, and physical learning and development, along with some very foundational knowledge. We now know with certainty, however, that children's literacy development also begins well before kindergarten.

For over 40 years, researchers have examined how young children begin to conceptualize print and how their early conceptualizations relate to the conventional literacy they will achieve with formal schooling. We understand that when exposed to print in their environments, most preschoolers will express curiosity about what it is and how it works. They will quite readily attempt to read the print they encounter—long before they understand exactly how print conveys meaning. Young children will also appropriate the written forms they see around them for use in their own drawing and writing. Many will proclaim that they are readers and writers well in advance of any conventional knowledge about what it is to read and write.

There was a time when preschool teachers could simply enjoy observing this literacy exploration, secure in the knowledge that responsibility for children's initial literacy learning was the purview of kindergarten or even first-grade teachers. That is no longer the case. Increasingly, preschools are held accountable for sending children to kindergarten "ready" for school, with readiness frequently described in terms of children's early literacy knowledge. Now, by the time they enter kindergarten, children are expected to recognize and name most of the letters of the alphabet, whether in uppercase or lowercase form. They are expected to have developed phonemic awareness and to have beginning understanding of the relationship between letters and sounds. In many communities, kindergarten teachers now can be fairly confident that on the first day of school, most children will be able to write their names—and perhaps many other common words.

While many preschool children will be naturally curious about print and will explore it on their own, not all children will be so inclined. Preschool teachers play a pivotal role in ensuring that *all* children achieve appropriate levels of early literacy before they move on to kindergarten. The way teachers structure their classrooms, the materials they choose to provide, the activities they facilitate, the lessons they plan, and the manner in which they interact with children throughout the day all impact the literacy of preschool children.

We offer *Reading and Writing in Preschool: Teaching the Essentials* to guide teachers as they support preschoolers' literacy learning and development. The primary focus of this book is supporting children's learning about print for both reading and writing. We recognize, of course, that preschoolers must focus on more than print if they are to become fully literate. The companion text in this series, *Oral Language and Comprehension in Preschool: Teaching the Essentials*, focuses on how to support children's language development for comprehension of stories and informational text. Together, the two texts offer a wealth of information that can enhance early literacy instruction in preschool.

This text begins with an overview of early literacy development, including explication of typical standards for preschool literacy. We then examine preschool contexts that support literacy learning and development, situating early literacy in both classroom and home environments. Particular attention is given to building bridges between home and school so that each context supports the other. The next chapter addresses the connections among oral language, reading, and writing, and offers strategies to support preschoolers' meaning making as they read and write both narrative and informational pieces. The use of technology to support early literacy is introduced here, and then carried through each subsequent chapter. The next two chapters present integrated and targeted strategies for helping children develop alphabetic knowledge for reading and writing. Integrated strategies like interactive reading and shared writing can be implemented across a school year to address multiple skills, while targeted strategies are designed to address very specific skills.

The final chapters are devoted to assessment of print knowledge for early reading and writing. Given the variability in knowledge and skill inherent in any preschool classroom, it is critically important that teachers plan experiences and activities that meet the needs of all children. That is best accomplished when teachers have a thorough understanding of what children do and do not know. Each assessment chapter begins with an overview of formal standardized assessments and describes their use in the preschool classroom. This is followed by a summary of reading and writing developmental milestones and strategies for ongoing observational assessment to document continued learning.

We hope that teachers with many different levels of experience—including those still in teacher preparation programs—will use this book to enhance their instructional practice. Throughout the book, we address myths about early literacy that have become entrenched in preschool programs, and we offer suggestions for reflecting on current practice in light of new understanding of preschool literacy. Like all preschool teachers, our goal is supporting children as they begin their journey to full literacy.

Acknowledgments

If it takes a village to raise a child, it also takes one to bring a book to fruition. We would first like to acknowledge all of the preschool teachers who have allowed us into their classrooms over the years. It is their stories that are reflected in these pages, and we thank them for their willingness to learn with us and often to serve as our teachers.

Special acknowledgment is in order for our colleague and friend Judith Schickedanz, now retired from Boston College. She was a coauthor with each of us for the two preschool literacy books on which this new title is based. Many of the vignettes and writing samples included here come from Judy's extensive collection drawn from her years of research in preschool classrooms and her pioneering work in early writing development.

Thanks also to faculty colleagues at Louisiana State University, Drs. Stan Barrera and Angela Webb. They read drafts of chapters and helped with final editing, including the tedious work of checking references. Finally, thank you to the staff at The Guilford Press for their support of this title and for their diligent attention to detail.

Contents

CHAPTER 1

Where Reading and Writing Begin

As another day begins, children arrive at their preschool. Four-year-old Gretchen stands in the doorway, head bowed, eyes aimed at the floor. Her mother nudges her gently and says, "Go ahead. Tell your teacher."

GRETCHEN: I got stitches. (*Walks through the doorway and turns her head to expose the right side of her chin.*)

TEACHER: (*Looks at stitches and also notices a bruise above her right eye.*) What happened, Gretchen?

GRETCHEN: I falled.

TEACHER: You fell? Did you fall someplace at your house, or did you fall at the park across the street?

GRETCHEN: In my room. And I can't jump on my bed anymore.

TEACHER: Oh, you fell while jumping on your bed?

GRETCHEN: I falled on the rocking chair.

TEACHER: Oh, you fell off your bed while jumping on it, and you hit the rocking chair?

GRETCHEN: I can't jump on the rocking chair anymore.

TEACHER: (*in an incredulous tone*) Did you try to jump from your bed to a rocking chair? (*Gretchen nods.*) Oh, my. So, you tried to jump into a rocking chair, and then what happened?

GRETCHEN: I, I, like this (*using hand motions to trace her fall's trajectory*), and then the . . . the . . . the rocking chair . . . the rocking chair, like this (*using hands again to indicate object falling over*), and the thing on the . . . that thing on the . . . on the bottom . . . the chair, the rocking chair hit my eye (*hand up to eye*) and my chin bumped the floor and bleeded (*hand on chin*), and then my mommy came and I had to sit in my car seat for the hospital.

TEACHER: So, you jumped up off your bed into the rocking chair, and then the rocking chair fell over, with you in it. When the rocking chair fell over, you fell onto the floor, and the bottom part that makes the chair rock hit you in the eye, and then your chin hit the floor. Is that what happened?

GRETCHEN: Yes, yes, and then I had to . . . had to . . . had to go to the hospital and they did stitches. My mommy took me.

TEACHER: Your mommy came to your room and then she took you to the hospital?

GRETCHEN: Yes, and my brother.

TEACHER: Oh, your brother went, too. Well, I'm sorry that you hurt yourself and had to have stitches. I bet you were scared.

GRETCHEN: Yes, I was.

TEACHER: That would be a wonderful story for our class book. Maybe you'd like to draw some pictures about falling and going to the hospital to get stitches, and I could write down what you say. Then, we could add this story to our class book. What do you think?

Gretchen does not answer. By this time, several children have gathered around to listen to the news, and Gretchen's best friend is clutching her hand. As the children head to a table to play, they continue talking about Gretchen's adventures the night before.

Gretchen's experience was a topic of conversation several times throughout the day. Other children told of similar experiences, and a hospital theme emerged in the dramatic play center. The children took the roles of parents, calling the doctor, taking sick children to the hospital, and warning about dangerous activities such as jumping on beds and running out into the street. As the children played, they created stories, pulling from their own experience to create fictionalized roles for themselves and the dolls serving as their "children."

UNDERSTANDING EARLY LITERACY

What do these conversations between Gretchen and her teacher and then with other children have to do with the emerging print knowledge that is the topic of this book? We would contend, "Everything!" For all children, literacy begins with language (Dickinson & Tabors, 2001). In fact, both reading and writing are particular specialized forms of language use.

Gretchen never composed a written account of her fall and stitches for the class book. Four-year-olds have a strong desire to tell all about something or to capture events in play, but less interest in creating a record of experiences once the story has been told or reenacted. They do not yet realize that written records help people save, recall, and share past experiences. However, Gretchen's teacher understood that talking about events and creating related scenarios in play help children like Gretchen to convey their intentions—their meanings. Although Gretchen did not actually record her experience in writing, these early social interactions with interested adults and peers help children learn to think and compose—an essential element in writing. And as children listen to the stories told by their teachers and friends, they learn how to extract meaning from the language of others—an essential element of reading. In fact, there is indisputable evidence that oral language and literacy learning are intricately connected (Biemiller, 2003; Burns, Griffin, & Snow, 1999; Dickinson & Porche, 2011; Pilonieta, Shue, & Kissel, 2014; Roskos, Tabors, & Lenhart, 2009; Scull, 2013).

Making Sense of Early Reading and Writing Processes

Certain areas of development have direct links to children's success in early reading and school readiness. Oral language, concepts of print, phonological awareness, and alphabet knowledge have strong scientifically based research support as predictors of early literacy success (National Early Literacy Panel [NELP], 2009; Snow, Burns, & Griffin, 1998). Some children are able to gain abilities in each of these as they interact with print in their environment and engage in extended language interactions with others, but most will need the assistance of knowledgeable adults who call their attention to specific aspects of written language. Gretchen's teacher did just that when she invited the child to create a page for the class book.

While the pages that follow will focus on children's developing awareness of print and the foundational concepts they must learn if they are to become successful independent readers and writers as they move through elementary school, it is important to keep in mind that literacy learning never happens in the absence of interesting things for children to read and write about. Children who practice naming and writing the alphabet letters through rote, repetitive activities devoid of any meaningful context are not likely to retain or apply their understanding of the alphabet over time. On the other hand, children who are excited to document for themselves and their parents the progression of stages they observe as a caterpillar metamorphoses into a butterfly will be eager to use their emerging knowledge of print so that they can share their new insights.

A well-equipped science and discovery center in a preschool classroom and a teacher's sharing of books related to the artifacts found there, for example, will prompt many children to engage with print in meaningful ways. Figure 1.1 shows a simple center created to accompany children's study of shadows and reflections within the *Opening the World of Learning* curriculum (Schickedanz & Dickinson, 2005). This center invites hands-on exploration of science concepts while also providing opportunities to engage with print through topically related picture books and writing materials. Classroom activities related to both science and social studies content can be especially enriching of children's knowledge bases and provide them with interesting ideas to read and write about. Rich, intriguing content is the key to meaningful reading and writing in preschool.

Standards for Early Literacy Learning

Teachers' awareness that children Gretchen's age need to be challenged to engage with print has emerged over time as standards for early literacy have been promulgated. Over the past few decades, there have been a number of standards movements aimed at improving academic achievement for children in American schools. Many of the early movements focused on achievement levels for children in elementary grades and high school. Over the past two decades, however, standards have also emerged for young children, particularly in the area of early literacy.

FIGURE 1.1. A thematic discovery center invites writing.

When they came to prominence the United States, preschools were seen primarily as a place to socialize young children into classroom culture. Thus, significant emphasis was placed on engaging children in free play for much of the day, albeit enhanced with educational materials typically not found in homes. Even as preschools came to be viewed as places to foster school readiness, notions of readiness were most often limited to helping children learn to use writing implements, recognize colors and shapes, and perhaps recite the alphabet and count from one to ten. Beginning in the 1990s, however, policymakers began to attend to the growing body of early literacy research demonstrating children's interest in and ability to learn about written language. The National Academy of Sciences was charged by the U.S. Congress to undertake an analysis of that body of research and mine it for scientifically supported practices that, if implemented appropriately, could prevent children from experiencing later reading difficulties (Snow et al., 1998).

Partly in response to that panel's efforts, the focus of early literacy research and preschool instruction shifted to much more intentional teaching of early literacy (Casbergue, 2010; McGee & Casbergue, 2011). Organizations such as the National Association for the Education of Young Children (NAEYC) and the International Reading Association (IRA) worked together to develop standards for early literacy learning and teaching (IRA & NAEYC, 1998) that fit within the framework of developmentally appropriate practice for young children (NAEYC, 2009). These standards encompassed a full range of literate behavior, including reading and writing.

The most recent standards movement in the United States led to the creation of the Common Core State Standards (CCSS; National Governors' Association & Center for Best Practices & Council of Chief School Officers [NGA & CCSSO], 2010). The CCSS language arts standards do not address learning in preschool, however, and focus most strongly on older children's comprehension of different kinds of texts, their ability to identify evidence for conclusions about what they read, and their understanding of sophisticated vocabulary. The CCSS standards for writing largely address older children's ability to compose essays in response to the fiction and nonfiction they read, and compose persuasive and argumentative texts. They do not address the early development of print concepts or children's emerging experimentation with composition that are the primary focus of this book.

While the CCSS do have potential to impact notions of school readiness, preschool teachers are much better served by looking to the national early literacy standards noted above and to the standards set out for young children by their own states or countries. Because this book focuses most closely on children's print knowledge and writing development, we do not specifically address the standards for language development, vocabulary knowledge, and reading comprehension. Those standards and strategies for supporting language, vocabulary, and comprehension development are addressed fully in the companion text in this series

(Roskos, Morrow, & Gambrell, in press). We have condensed information from many sets of early literacy standards related to learning about print in Table 1.1 to illustrate typical standards and learning experiences for supporting preschool children's development of print concepts.

Concepts of Print

The term *concepts of print* refers to children's knowledge of the functions of print and how print works. This includes an understanding that books are read from front to back; an awareness of how print is placed on a page; and an understanding that print carries meaning, has a variety of uses or functions in our lives, and is speech written down. In order to make sense of print, one also needs to understand directionality and comprehend both the concept of word (words are composed of letters and separated by spaces) and the concept of letter (letters have distinct shapes, have names, and form words). Teachers help children learn these concepts through repeated exposure to and guided activities with books, charts, Big Books, and various types of functional print, and through demonstrating writing and inviting children themselves to write. Her teacher's suggestion that Gretchen create a page for a class book was one such invitation.

TABLE 1.1. Typical Standards and Learning Experiences: Concepts of Print

Standards	Learning experiences
• Understands that print is used for different functions. • Understands that speech can be written down. • Understands that print carries a message. • Understands that illustrations carry meaning but cannot be read. • Understands that books have titles and authors. • Understands concepts of word—letters are grouped to form words, and words are separated by spaces. • Understands concept of directionality—front to back, left to right, and top to bottom movement on a page. • Understands that letters function differently than numbers.	• Observes varied uses of print for various purposes (e.g., shopping lists, recipes, and other simple directions, and letters and messages) and participates in their creation and use. • Observes adults writing as they say the words aloud (write aloud). • Participates in composing process by offering ideas and language for others to write down. • Attends to print during Big Book activities. • Refers to books by their titles; is beginning to understand that a book represents a person's ideas and that this person is the author. • Engages in opportunities to draw and "write" independently. • Observes and follows along as adults track print from left to right while reading aloud; browses through books from front to back. • Participates in opportunities to write his or her own name and brief messages.

Phonemic Awareness

Phonemic awareness is the ability to hear, identify, and manipulate the individual sounds (phonemes) in spoken words. It is one level of phonological awareness, the general understanding that words consist of sounds. Phonemic awareness requires more specific skills than other levels of phonological awareness; these skills link more directly to phonics, which relates sounds to the letters that represent them. Instruction in phonemic awareness may, at times, involve the use of print. That is, it may include linking a letter or letters to sounds in spoken words as they are stressed or isolated by an adult.

Children demonstrate their knowledge of the beginning levels of phonological awareness when they:

- Identify and make oral rhymes (e.g., "I can bake a chocolate [cake]." "The cat wore a [hat].")
- Identify and work with syllables in spoken words (e.g., Jess [one clap], Becky [two claps]).

Children demonstrate their knowledge of finer aspects of phonological awareness (phonemic awareness) when they:

- Identify and work with onsets and rimes in one-syllable words (e.g., the first part of *dog* is /d/: the last part of *cat* is /at/).
- Attempt to write words by using a letter to represent a sound heard in the word (e.g., *b* for *baby*, *o* for *ghost*).
- Recognize when several words begin with the same sound (e.g., "Wee Willie went walking"; "Peter Piper picked a peck of pickled peppers").
- Identify words that begin with a specific sound (e.g., match and sort pictures according to initial sound).

Phonemic awareness activities are most effective when children are taught to manipulate phonemes and to anchor or code these phonemes with letters. This is sometimes referred to as "phonological awareness with a phonics connection" (Armbruster, Lehr, & Osborn, 2003; Piasta & Wagner, 2010). Table 1.2 shows typical standards and learning experiences for supporting preschool children's development of phonemic awareness.

Alphabet Knowledge

Letter name knowledge, or alphabet knowledge, is an excellent predictor of success in early reading. The fluency (accuracy and speed) with which children recognize letters gives them an advantage in learning to read. Letter names are part of the language used to talk about reading and writing. Alphabet knowledge often

TABLE 1.2. Typical Standards and Learning Experiences: Phonemic Awareness

Standards	Learning experiences
• Builds on understandings associated with phonological awareness, such as ability to recognize and produce words starting with the same sound. • Has the general understanding that letters represent the sounds that make up spoken words (alphabetic principle). • Begins to make some sound–letter associations.	• Observes others as they segment spoken words into their individual sounds and use letters to write the sounds. • Selects letters to represent individual sounds that a teacher has segmented in a spoken word. • Selects a letter to represent an individual sound (usually at the beginning of a word) that he or she has segmented in a spoken word.

indicates children's interest in learning how letters and sounds relate to one another and helps them remember how words are spelled. Some researchers suggest that alphabet knowledge is a by-product of extensive early literacy experiences. Therefore, simply training children to recite the alphabet or memorize letters without providing learning in a larger literacy context has proven unsuccessful as a predictor of beginning reading success (Anderson, Hiebert, Scott, & Wilkinson, 1985; Piasta & Wagner, 2010).

According to Burns and colleagues (1999), "By the end of kindergarten, children should be able to name most of the letters of the alphabet, no matter what order they come in, no matter if they are uppercase or lowercase. And they should do it quickly and effortlessly" (p. 80). At the preschool level, children are now generally expected to know *at least* 19 uppercase letters as indicated by the most recent benchmarks set by the federal Early Reading First initiative (U.S. Department of Education, 2015). Often children attend first to the letters in their own names. Parents and teachers should expand children's knowledge of the alphabet by providing opportunities for children to learn letter names as part of a variety of rich literacy and oral language experiences. Table 1.3 shows typical standards and learning experiences for supporting preschool children's development of alphabet knowledge.

BALANCING ATTENTION TO PRINT AND MEANING

This book focuses on how preschool children develop knowledge about print that they will eventually use to read and write independently. While we specifically target print knowledge, it is important to keep in mind that literacy is language. Reading and writing are attempts to extract and convey meaning using symbols on a page. It does a child little good to recite letters of the alphabet if he or she doesn't know what letters actually are or how they are used to understand and convey

TABLE 1.3. Typical Standards and Learning Experiences: Alphabet Knowledge

Standards	Learning experiences
• Notices and is able to name letters that begin common logos and names of friends and family members. • Understands that letters of the alphabet are special visual graphics that have unique names. • Identifies at least 19 upper-case letters of the alphabet. • Identifies at least 12 lower-case letters of the alphabet. • Identifies letters in his or her own name.	• Uses magnetic letters or tiles for play and exploration; plays with alphabet puzzles. • Has experiences with alphabet books. • Discusses letter names in the context of daily meaningful activities. • Observes and participates in experiences where letter names are linked to writing names and other meaningful words.

messages. And while children certainly need to recognize and form the letters of the alphabet, it is equally important for them to learn how to use those letters to share their thoughts.

Young children themselves intuitively balance their attention to print and meaning. Preschoolers often create large quantities of writing that involve no composing. When children write without composing, they simply explore the physical forms of writing. Figure 1.2 shows writing of this kind created by a 4-year-old. When the teacher asked the child to tell her about his writing, the child said, "It's nothing." Apparently, the child was simply practicing some of the letters in his name (*ADAM*), or stringing letters together to create something that looked like writing, not attempting to communicate a specific message.

In another example, Figure 1.3 is a single page of a 14-page "storybook" written by another 4-year-old. Although the child said it was a storybook, it had

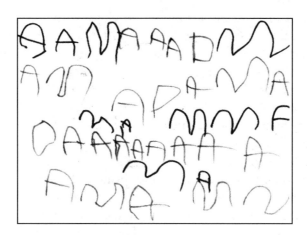

FIGURE 1.2. Writing without composing.

FIGURE 1.3. A preschooler's page of a storybook.

no specific story. This child, too, was simply creating an artifact that resembled a storybook. He even drew a line down the center of each sheet of paper to indicate where the bound pages of an actual book come together!

Figure 1.4 is a child's experiment in making a lot of letters and letter-like forms, none of which represented any thoughts. Figure 1.5 shows a child's "words," which were not any words in particular. These mock words were the products of the 4-year-old's experimentation with putting letters together to make collections that look like words.

Creating print markings is a skill that develops in conjunction with a child's budding picture-making skills. Development in both domains proceeds by leaps and bounds between 3 and 5 years of age. Three-year-olds, especially, often combine both writing and picture marks in the same performance. As Howard Gardner noted in *Artful Scribbles: The Significance of Children's Drawings* (1980), these combination pieces typically do not convey a message. Instead, children use these to inventory many of the graphic forms they have in their repertoires. Figures 1.6a and 1.6b are examples of this kind of performance. Each was produced by a different young 3-year-old.

At the same time that children explore print and drawing simply to experiment with graphics, they are keenly interested in messages. They love to hear favorite books read aloud over and over, reveling in the humor of stories, eagerly reciting familiar refrains, and puzzling over how a beloved character might solve a thorny problem. They want to know what words in their environment mean, and

FIGURE 1.4. Experimentation with letters and letter-like forms.

FIGURE 1.5. A preschooler's experimentation with words.

FIGURE 1.6. Preschoolers often combine drawing and writing.

they demand that adults read to them. The pleasure both teachers and children can derive from reading together is evident in Figure 1.7.

Preschoolers who understand that the print and illustrations in books have meaning also expect that their own writing can have meaning, even if they don't know what that meaning might be. Anyone who has worked with preschoolers knows the charming frustration of being asked by a child what his page full of scribbles and random letters "says." With appropriate support and modeling, preschoolers come to understand that actual messages can be written down, and that once written, those messages will always convey the same idea. This often results in requests for help creating notes and signs that can be used to convey children's important messages, whether those messages are expressions of affection for parents or pets, or prohibitions against knocking down a carefully constructed block structure.

Preschoolers' attention to both print for its own sake and to the meaning behind it underscores their natural inclination to balance attention to both print and meaning. Teachers need to nurture children's interest in both!

BRIDGING THE ORAL AND GRAPHIC WORLDS

From these descriptions of how children attend to and experiment with print, it should be apparent that one of the major tasks of literacy development for preschoolers is bridging from oral to written language. Gretchen's interaction with

FIGURE 1.7. Children are keenly interested in messages, whether they are reading or writing.

her teacher illustrated that children might have a lot of information they want to share, but at first they do so through oral language only. When preschoolers do use marks to convey meaning, whether in the pictures they draw or in the scribble writing they create, they often must tell us what their marks "say"—what they mean. Preschoolers cannot at first capture all of their thoughts and feelings in graphic form—their pictures and writing at first fall short of the conventional, and cannot easily be interpreted by others. Only with the help of their verbal explanations can others find out about preschoolers' intended meanings.

Beginning during the preschool years and continuing through kindergarten and the primary grades, children gradually become more skilled in both drawing and writing. Little by little, the marks children put on a page begin to stand more on their own to represent the messages they wish to convey. In this way, the graphic world becomes a bridge to the oral world because drawings and writing capture more of the meaning a child tries to communicate.

In a similar vein, when preschoolers first interact with books, they do not extract meaning conventionally from the print. In fact, their attempts to read are usually governed by pictures. Initially, they are unaware that the print on a page carries any meaning. It is not uncommon for children to inadvertently cover print with their hands as they lean in to look at pictures while someone reads to them. As far as they know, an adult reading a book need only look at the pictures to tell the story! They may be completely unaware of the print on each page.

Thus, the teacher's job is to expand children's awareness of print and help them make connections between oral and written language. In the following chapters, we accompany children on their journey from oral language to the beginnings of reading and writing. Actually, several journeys are described. As we have already suggested, a child's literacy development rests on the gradual coming together of various strands of knowledge and skills. One journey involves the child's first steps in moving from oral language and pictures to writing and reading print. Other journeys involve the child's movement from scribbles to recognizable alphabet letters, and from strings of letters to actual words created through growing awareness of phonological principles. There is also the journey from the understanding and creation of short, simple messages to messages that are reasonably detailed and coherent.

Subsequent chapters explore in detail the role of preschool teachers in helping children along these journeys. As the journeys are described, information about the settings in which reading and writing take place, and about the importance of support from both materials and people will be provided. Children must be assisted in many ways in making their journeys, if the story is to end as we would hope, with competent children, excited about books, full of ideas and eager to record them, and confident in their ability to read and write.

Most names used in this book are pseudonyms, except when we have obtained parents' permission to use children's images and writing artifacts. Descriptions of students and teachers are composite sketches that represent real classroom situations that we have encountered in our studies.

Myths about Preschool Literacy

Preschool is too early to begin literacy instruction; young children are not ready to learn about print.

In this book, we demonstrate that children actually are keenly interested in print and very eager to learn to use it for their own purposes. Withholding opportunities for children to learn about print diminishes their interest and prevents them from developing age-appropriate skills that will contribute significantly to their ongoing literacy learning.

Preschool children should be allowed to spend all of their time playing. That is how young children learn.

It is true that play is a primary means by which young children learn. That does not negate the need for skillful guidance to shape children's interactions with print even as they play. Many of the strategies we describe in subsequent chapters offer ideas for enhancing children's play by providing opportunities for them to incorporate reading and writing into their play, and especially into their pretence. It is also true that even 4-year-olds participate with interest and attention in brief periods of explicit instruction, particularly in individual or small-group settings. We detail a number of playful lessons that teach children about print, as well as ideas for incorporating print knowledge into activities that transition children from one classroom event to the next. We honor the right of children to play, and demonstrate how developmentally appropriate literacy activities can extend and enhance their play.

Children need to be able to read before we expect them to write.

The brief overview of literacy development in this chapter illustrates that the journeys children embark on as they become both readers and writers are basically the same. Their primary task is to learn how oral and written language are connected. To do so, they explore how print works—how to recognize their names to locate their cubbies, how to write their own names to claim paintings they want to bring home, how to read simple lines of print in a morning message, or how to compose their own messages. They are as eager to write as they are to read, and print knowledge learned through one medium enhances the other.

IDEAS FOR DISCUSSION, REFLECTION, AND ACTION

1. Does your state, district, or school have preschool standards? If so, what are expectations for concepts of print, phonemic awareness, and alphabet knowledge, and how are you and your colleagues addressing them? Reflect on your classroom. Discuss the learning opportunities available in each category with your colleagues. Which items do you feel confident about? Which items need more attention? Use Tables 1.1, 1.2, and 1.3 as a guide.

2. The need to maintain developmentally appropriate practice while addressing accountability often leads educators to take sides between "what is best for children" and "what will further children's ability to demonstrate what they have learned." The discussion tends to dichotomize the way people think about literacy learning and promote misunderstandings about the distinction between what is important to teach and how it should be taught. Is this a point of tension in your school? If so, talk about what it means for helping children learn about print.

3. Widely accepted best practices in early childhood literacy education suggest that effective early childhood literacy programs:

   - Are grounded in what is known about children's physical, social, emotional, and cognitive development.
   - Are planful and intentional.
   - Acknowledge and value differences among children.
   - Involve scaffolding children's experiences from the known to the unknown.
   - Engage children in ways that are meaningful and pleasurable.
   - Are developmentally appropriate.

   Read these descriptions and discuss them with your colleagues. What might these practices mean for your program?

4. As you review and discuss the language and literacy standards for your school or district, discuss ways to address them in an integrated way through content of interest to children. Social studies and science content provide an excellent vehicle for expanding children's background knowledge and their language and literacy skills. Try out some of the ideas discussed and share them with others.

5. Continue to follow up with the discussion regarding the need to reconcile perceived tension between developmentally appropriate practice and the demands for demonstrated progress. How are you and your colleagues maintaining an atmosphere of enjoyment and engagement in the literacy activities in which children are involved?

CHAPTER 2

Preschool Contexts for Literacy Development and Learning

Four-year-old Keviana noticed a visitor examining the different centers in her classroom and promptly went over to offer a tour, chatting about what she liked to do in each area. As she animatedly described how she and her friends play princesses in the housekeeping center, she paused to contemplate one of the printed labels her teacher had placed on the furnishings. Running her finger under the word *refrigerator*, she announced, "This word is 'frigerator!" She wasn't quite satisfied with her reading, though, whispering, "That's a lot of letters." After a brief pause, she said cheerfully, "It says 'frigerator to keep food cold!"

Undoubtedly like most preschool children, Keviana is keenly attuned to her surroundings. Her conversation with the visitor reveals that she is aware of how her classroom is organized and the purpose of each area. She also notices and carefully attends to the print she encounters there. While her reading of that print is not yet conventional, her interpretation of the word *refrigerator* illustrates that she knows quite a lot about print and how it works. She is aware that labels often function to name the objects to which they are attached, but that they may also indicate additional information. She understands the concepts of "words" and "letters," that is, that a collection of letters appearing together without spaces can be a word. At the same time, she isn't completely sure whether that collection of letters is a single word or perhaps a phrase. What matters most, though, is that Keviana is interested in the print found in her environment and actively engages with that environmental print.

One important way that children construct knowledge about print is through interactions with logos, labels, road signs, and other meaningful visual displays found in their environment. Children observe as adults use environmental print in functional ways (e.g., to choose from a menu, to stop at a stop sign, to select products at the supermarket, or to order pizza online). Children who understand how print functions in their lives are more apt to be curious about how written language works. They develop a growing interest in words and letters, and they are likely to ask questions about what written words say. Sometimes children make use of these meaningful symbols as they choose a particular kind of juice from the refrigerator or return classroom materials to a bin with a picture and printed label. Their emerging awareness of how print functions is a key motivating force for learning to read and write.

Whether engaging with print at home, in their neighborhoods, or in classrooms, it is clear that children's environments can significantly impact their literacy development. In this chapter, we explore children's interactions with print across multiple environments, and offer strategies for encouraging use of print in classrooms and at home.

PROVIDING PRINT-RICH CLASSROOM ENVIRONMENTS

It is not enough that children learn to notice print in their environment. They must understand the uses and functions of print in their daily lives, both inside and outside of school. Effective teachers plan the classroom environment so that children regularly engage in interpreting and using meaningful symbols. In this section, we address how to plan for and implement three important aspects of the classroom environment: (1) print exposure and use, (2) literacy materials, and (3) adult–child interaction.

Print Exposure and Use

In print-rich classrooms, opportunities for using print emerge throughout the day. Functional print in the classroom, such as names on children's cubbies or labels on shelves to indicate where materials belong, invites children to engage with meaningful print that serves a clear purpose. Thus, gathering jackets from the correct cubbies before heading outside or putting away treasured art creations to take home at the end of the day become opportunities to make use of print. So too does clean-up time when children transition from free play in centers to the next classroom activity.

In addition, effective teachers plan specific activities to make use of the print to which children are exposed. Some of these activities are embedded in daily routines such as having children sign in as they enter the classroom or using name cards to take attendance. Morning messages that children and teachers read together as they gather to start each day have become ubiquitous in preschool classrooms and, if used effectively (Wasik & Hindman, 2011), also encourage children's engagement with print.

Other activities result from special experiences. For example, a trip to a farmers' market might inspire a chart listing the things children think they will see. Vocabulary words such as *vegetables* and *plants* might be labeled with pictures so that children begin to associate written words with their meanings. After the visit, photographs of children at the market with their dictated explanations of what they were doing and their drawings about their experience can be placed on a bulletin board that is sure to attract children's interest and spark conversations among them as they retell their experience while examining the pictures and print. Figure 2.1 illustrates a bulletin board display documenting one multi-age preschool/kindergarten classroom's end-of-the-year visit to the Crescent City Farmers' Market.

Classroom teachers must also consider children's exposure to and use of print in digital forms. Definitions of literacy have expanded to acknowledge meaning making in many forms, including web searches, text messaging, and e-mail as well as nonprint media such as animations, video, and photos (Lankshear & Knobel, 2006, 2011). Children routinely see adults in their communities engage in literate behavior using all of these forms, and it is not uncommon for even young children to experiment with technology as a means of acquiring new forms of literacy (Wohlwend, 2010). Children's awareness and use of multiple forms of literacy can be enhanced as they participate in digital communication, as when a teacher invites a child to the classroom computer and says, "Let's e-mail your mom a reminder that she is bringing our snack tomorrow!" Children can also be invited to engage in teacher-led Internet searches related to classroom activities and outings. In preparation for a visit to the firehouse, for example, the teacher could conduct a search for images of different types of firefighting equipment as children follow along on an interactive whiteboard talking about what they find and predicting what they will see when they visit the neighborhood firefighters. While children will be focused on interesting content and images, they will also gain exposure to the idea of seeking information on the Internet and see that process in action (Lisenbee, 2009). Figure 2.2 offers guidelines for print exposure and use.

Classroom Materials

Careful selection and placement of materials can make a big difference in how well children make use of the classroom environment to learn about print. Materials should allow children to make choices, work independently or with others to complete a task, and develop both creativity and print-related skills. Materials for reading, drawing, and writing should be available in many areas of the classroom.

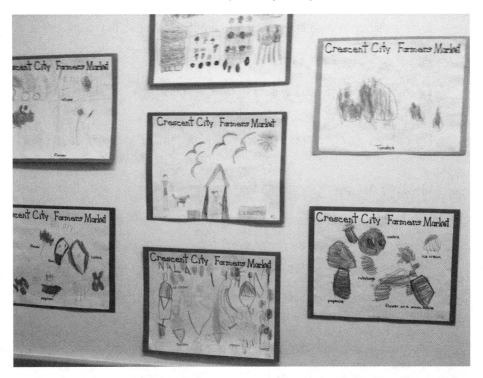

FIGURE 2.1. Farmers' market bulletin board display.

_____ Print is visible on open charts and bulletin boards around the room.

_____ Print is incorporated in each area of the classroom.

_____ Environmental print is clear, easy to read, and displayed at children's eye level.

_____ Environmental print represents words that are familiar to children because of daily activities, thematic inquiries, and special experiences.

_____ Children's names are printed on their cubbies, placements, and other items.

_____ Name cards and other carefully printed words are available for children to copy or "read."

_____ Children are encouraged to write their own names or letters from their names on their paintings and drawings.

_____ Some print is written in language other than English.

_____ Mailboxes are available for each child and family, encouraging communication between home and school and showing children that written messages are an integral part of classroom life.

_____ A newsletter describing children's activities is shared with the children and sent home regularly.

_____ Children see forms of digital communication such as e-mail and text messages used between parents and teachers.

_____ Children are encouraged to explore print in multiple forms including print books and e-books, computer programs, and print apps using tablet technology.

FIGURE 2.2. Checklist for print exposure and use.

Table 2.1 offers examples of many kinds of materials that promote awareness of shapes, forms, and symbols—awareness that is critical to children's eventual understanding of print. These materials can be spread across many centers, including dramatic play centers, the writing center, the library center, the art center, and the area for tabletop games and puzzles.

While most well-equipped preschool classrooms have always included markers, crayons, and paper in art areas, dedicated writing and word play centers are also necessary. These centers are expressly devoted to children's exploration of print and writing. They serve as an area where children know they can find what they need when they want to make a sign, create an invitation to a pretend party, or write a note to be placed in the classroom mailbox for delivery to a classmate. In addition to writing materials, these centers should contain alphabet puzzles, magnetic letters, sets of cards with each child's picture and name, and letter stamps. Magnetic boards, small dry-erase or chalk boards, paper, cards, and construction paper of all different colors and sizes invite children to experiment with writing and play with print.

Computer stations and iPad or other electronic tablets placed in centers offer further opportunities for children to explore print (Northrop & Killeen, 2013). There are many computer programs and tablet applications (apps) that allow children to follow print as electronic books are read aloud and even to create their own e-books with teacher assistance. Simple writing programs offer further options for experimentation. Many apps also include games that allow children to manipulate letters on the screen, moving them to sort by sounds or create words, for example. For some children, tablet technology is more appealing than engaging in similar activities with more traditional materials like print books, word cards, and letter tiles (Larson, 2010).

TABLE 2.1. Materials and Activities That Promote Awareness of Shapes, Forms, and Symbols

Materials	Activities
• ABC and number books	• Classifying
• Alphabet boards (for matching)	• Comparing
• Alphabet cards	• Differentiating by color, shape, and
• iPads and computers	size
• Board games (lotto, bingo)	• Drawing and writing
• Chalkboards and chalk	• Matching
• Class books	• Pairing
• Dominoes (with pictures for younger children)	• Patterning
• Magnetic letters and magnet boards	• "Reading" and independent
• Assorted paper for writing and drawing	browsing
• Picture dictionaries	• Sequencing
• Pictures of objects to pair, match, and classify	
• Writing utensils	

In addition to dedicated writing and print exploration centers, writing implements and materials should be infused into dramatic play centers. Preschoolers' dramatic play offers a potent opportunity for exploration of print. A veterinarian's office (or a shoe store, restaurant, or bakery), if equipped with relevant literacy props, will prompt use of print. The vet's office, for example, could include prescription pads, receipts, an appointment book, and a notepad for writing instructions for follow-up care. Actual artifacts of print material and signs from a real veterinary office will provide models that children can imitate. Empty boxes of heartworm medication and flea treatments, or clean empty bottles of pet shampoo and vitamin supplements, for example, will infuse the center with print that children will naturally attend to as they examine pets and prescribe treatments.

Figure 2.3 is an example of the kind of writing that can result when preschool dramatic play centers are equipped with appropriate writing materials. Among literacy props in Hannah's classroom housekeeping center were a notepad and a small bulletin board on the "kitchen" counter. Hannah and her friends were getting ready to go out for the evening, which included leaving their children with a babysitter. Hannah began a note to the babysitter by writing the name of her child, "Ben" (actually the name of her older brother—a very familiar word). She then explained that she could be reached at the phone number on the first line. Note that she did not write her real phone number but rather something visually similar to a phone number, suggesting knowledge of a form most likely observed in her environment. The phone number contained six digits, although the final symbol was a letter not a number. The remaining lines of apparent scribble were instructions for feeding the baby and putting him to bed. Hannah confided that she wrote the instructions in script like her mommy's handwriting. Clearly the dramatic play center and one of the writing props included functioned to bring an opportunity for Hannah to use her knowledge of environmental print to compose personally meaningful writing that furthered her play.

FIGURE 2.3. Hannah's note to the babysitter.

If children are to make use of reading and writing materials, teachers need to plan carefully for inclusion of those print materials into dramatic play centers. To decide what materials to include, first consider the roles that children are likely to assume depending on the theme of the center. In a doctor's office, for example, children might pretend to be patients, parents escorting sick children, doctors, nurses, or receptionists. Next, consider the kinds of printed materials adults in those roles might use and add those authentic print examples to the center. For the medical center, this might include health and wellness brochures and magazines typically found in waiting rooms, patient charts, prescription pads, insurance forms, and receipts. Finally, provide appropriate props and simplified versions of those authentic print materials for children to incorporate into their play. Table 2.2 offers an example of a completed plan for supporting print awareness and writing in an outdoor dramatic play center, an environment that is often overlooked as teachers plan for children's play! This planning guide can be used each time the theme of a dramatic play center changes.

Children can also be prompted to incorporate reading and writing into their block play. Time in a block center often includes considerable dramatic play, as children build pretend skyscrapers, houses, and hospitals, and use miniature cars, trucks, police cruisers, ambulances, and play figures to enact scenes from city life. If materials are readily available, it is common for preschoolers to supplement model traffic signs with their own handwritten ones and to create labels for buildings and streets. Children also sometimes create bus tickets, and "do not enter" or "open" and "closed" signs to support their block play. Simply placing markers and appropriately sized paper, tongue depressors, and masking tape in the block center is sometimes enough to encourage writing for these purposes.

Adult–Child Interaction

Children's learning flourishes when they are involved in nurturing relationships with caring and responsible adults (Cabell et al., 2011; Mashburn et al., 2008; Pakarinen et al., 2014). Such adults not only plan opportunities for children to

TABLE 2.2. Guidelines for Planning Print-Enhanced Dramatic Play Centers

Theme	Tricycle path/gas station/car repair shop
Roles	Driver, car wash attendant, police officer, mechanic, gas station attendant, car inspection officer
Authentic print materials	Car care brochures, owner's manuals, advertisements for batteries and tires, circulars from local auto parts stores
Children's materials and props	Order forms, receipts, inspection tags, repair logs, checks, traffic ticket forms, tools, hoses for pretend car washing and tire inflation

learn about print, but they also take advantage of children's natural curiosity about the print in their environment. They answer children's questions, extend their understanding, and prompt new learning whenever the opportunities occur. Highly skilled teachers recognize children's inclination to incorporate reading and writing into their play and actively support and extend their experimentation by enriching environmental print to match children's interests. They are also aware that they sometimes need to model use of print materials in order to nudge children to do the same.

In the midst of the construction boom that followed a hurricane in one community, for example, a teacher noticed that children were very aware of the large numbers of construction workers gathered each morning in the parking lot of a nearby building supply store. She considered setting up a construction supply store as a dramatic play area in which children could work through their ideas about the jobs of the workers they saw every day. She realized, however, that the block center was already serving that purpose as the children acted out stopping at the store (the block shelves) to select lumber and tools before heading to their "job sites."

She capitalized on the children's interests by sharing nonfiction picture books about construction, and placing those books in the block center. She engaged children in a shared writing activity in which they created lists of building supplies and construction equipment. Finally, she joined the children in the block center as they played, using writing materials already there to model writing out an order for building supplies. She also drew a simple plan for rebuilding a garage—a frequently seen construction project in the area around the school. The children

FIGURE 2.4. Tyler writing in the block center.

quickly joined in, filling her order with blocks and tools and then helping her build her garage. Almost immediately after she left her order form and plan on the top of the block shelf, children began to use her models to create orders of their own before selecting blocks. Figure 2.4 shows 4-year-old Tyler in the process of doing just that. Over the next few weeks, children's own lists of supplies and plans for buildings filled the block area.

Even though Tyler's block center writing was mostly conventional in form—real words copied from the teacher's model—it is important to remember that many children use scribble writing or strings of letters when they write, especially as part of dramatic play. Frequently, the writing children do in dramatic play is not intended to represent a specific message. Rather, writing is simply part of acting out a pretend scenario that emulates adult activities, not much different from cooking and serving pretend meals. Pretending to create an order form is much more important to the play than what the form actually says.

This example of one teacher's engagement with children during their play illustrates the powerful influence adults can have on children's eagerness to incorporate reading and writing into their everyday activities. Figure 2.5 offers general guidelines for print- and learning-related adult–child interaction.

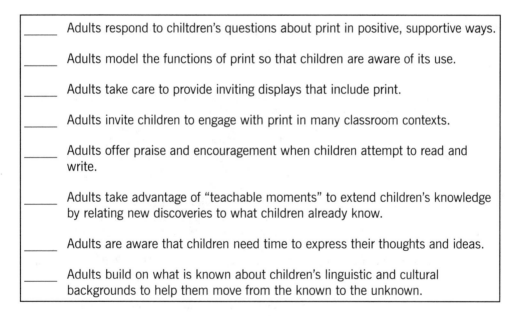

_____ Adults respond to chiltdren's questions about print in positive, supportive ways.

_____ Adults model the functions of print so that children are aware of its use.

_____ Adults take care to provide inviting displays that include print.

_____ Adults invite children to engage with print in many classroom contexts.

_____ Adults offer praise and encouragement when children attempt to read and write.

_____ Adults take advantage of "teachable moments" to extend children's knowledge by relating new discoveries to what children already know.

_____ Adults are aware that children need time to express their thoughts and ideas.

_____ Adults build on what is known about children's linguistic and cultural backgrounds to help them move from the known to the unknown.

FIGURE 2.5. Checklist of guidelines for adult–child interaction.

In addition to supporting children's experimentation with print during daily routines and while they play, well-planned early literacy programs also have structures that allow for differentiated instruction; that is, teachers meet with the whole group, with small groups, or with individuals depending on the activity. The younger children are, the more they need one-on-one adult attention, but this will not happen automatically (Schickedanz, 2003). Ironically, programs that have a tightly organized underlying structure are more likely to yield a fluid, comfortable daily schedule for children. This requires considerable forethought and cooperation among staff. Table 2.3 provides some general guidelines for planning differentiated instruction.

SUPPORTING PRINT-RICH HOME ENVIRONMENTS

Just as children benefit from opportunities to notice and experiment with print in preschool classrooms, their literacy development is enhanced if they also are immersed in print at home. While teachers obviously have little control over children's home environments, they can assist parents in recognizing the importance

TABLE 2.3. Guidelines for Organizing Groups for Differentiated Instruction

Organizational pattern	Interactions
Whole class	
• Generally occurs once or twice a day; includes read-aloud time, interactive writing, phonological awareness activities, and letter knowledge activities.	• Explicit instruction in content to which all children should be exposed • Intentional; builds on stated curriculum goals • Used diagnostically to determine the need for individual and small-group follow-up instruction
Small group	
• Should be scheduled for 10–15 minute period every day, with the teacher and assistant each leading a group. • May occur as part of center-time activities.	• Follow-up to whole-class activity • Scaffolded explicit print instruction • Opportunity to revisit specific aspects of whole-class activity with two or three children (e.g., "Did you notice any letters that looked the same on our chart?") • Intervention for English language learners, educationally advanced children, and children with other special needs
One on one	
• May occur during center time or as brief, highly focused adult–child interactions throughout the day.	• Same as small-group instruction, only individualized

of engaging preschoolers in age-appropriate reading and writing and the benefits of inviting children to share in their own everyday use of print (Paratore, 2011; Paratore & Edwards, 2011). Although all parents want their children to succeed in school, some may be unaware of the importance of specific types of literacy interactions at home that are most likely to support children's early literacy learning. This is especially true of families living in immigrant or other nonmainstream communities in which parents may engage children with print in ways that differ significantly from approaches used by teachers (Robins, Treiman, Rosales, & Otake, 2012; Wessels & Trainin, 2014).

While teachers need to share their knowledge about how parents can support early literacy at home, it is equally important for teachers to invite families to share their observations of children's literacy outside of school. Doing so enables teachers to broaden their understanding of children's preferences for reading and writing and perhaps adapt classroom activities accordingly (Baroody & Dobbs-Oates, 2011). Acknowledging that parents have significant insight into their own children's learning and that all communities provide rich environments that reflect families' culture honors the "funds of knowledge" from which all children can draw (Gonzales, Moll, & Amanti, 2005).

Materials for Home Literacy

Most homes are filled with print! Unlike dramatic play areas in classrooms where environmental print often references "pretend" items—plastic food, empty containers, make- believe checks and receipts—almost all print at home is functional. Pantries and refrigerators are filled with actual food products in original packaging with which children are intimately familiar. Ask any parent what happens if an attempt is made to substitute a new cereal for the child's favorite! Simply bringing out the new and unfamiliar box at breakfast may induce howls of protest even before the cereal inside is actually visible. When that happens, children are responding to meaningful environmental print. They recognize the logos on the things they like, and are quick to take in new and unfamiliar logos that signal a change they may not be willing to make.

Many homes contain a note pad near the pantry where parents routinely jot down items they will need to buy during their next trip to the grocery. Message pads are often situated beside the telephone for taking messages. In many households, a calendar on which appointments, athletic practices, and after school activities are written as they are scheduled is indispensible. And as the parents have become increasingly aware of the importance of reading with and to young children, books and magazines are often available for children's use.

All of these items have potential for engaging children in exploration of print at home. Just as teachers need to model print use and nudge children to experiment with it in the classroom, parents may also need to intentionally draw their children into functional uses of print at home. Teachers need to be aware of opportunities to help parents recognize the importance of calling children's attention to the print that naturally surrounds them at home and offer suggestions for activities like encouraging preschoolers to help with creating the grocery list or writing items on the calendar. They can help parents understand that allowing children to see them read and write at home and inviting children's participation will go a long way toward supporting literacy learning, with no specialized training required.

Strategies for Connecting Home and School

Fully engaging all of the adults in children's lives in supporting preschoolers' literacy development acknowledges that all families have strengths and can help their children achieve (Amaro-Jiménez & Semingson, 2011). As teachers communicate with parents and other caregivers about children's literacy development, they gain insight into how home environments and family situations help shape each child's learning. Understanding children's literacy environments outside of school allows teachers to acknowledge and encourage parents' efforts while also providing suggestions for additional ways print exploration can be supported at home.

It is relatively easy for teachers to enlist parents' help in gathering information that will increase their understanding of children's literacy development. In both home and school settings, children's reading and writing behavior can be observed, with examples then shared and discussed. Teachers can encourage parents to watch for any signs of drawing and writing by children at home and to share samples and information about what they observed with teachers at school. Hannah's mother brought the sample shown in Figure 2.6 to school. She had watched and listened

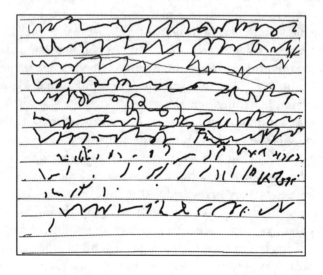

FIGURE 2.6. Hannah's meeting notes.

while Hannah gathered stuffed animals and dolls, conducted a meeting, and took notes on a stenographer's pad, borrowed from her mom's desk.

Hannah's meeting "minutes" are a series of linear scribbles. During a brief interaction with Hannah's mother when she dropped the child off at school, Hannah's teacher was able to point out that Hannah knew that writing was created in lines, from left to right, and that writing could be used to write down things to be remembered, such as an important discussion at a meeting.

Not long after this, Hannah's mom sent in the sample shown in Figure 2.7 with a note that said, "Hannah had another meeting." When Hannah's mother picked her up that afternoon, she also pointed out to the teacher that Hannah had attempted to write her name at the top of the page. The teacher then noted that unlike in the first sample, Hannah had written a series of separate figures this time. Her writing behavior suggested that she had made an important discovery: that print is composed of distinct letters.

Hannah's teacher also drew the mother's attention to what appeared to be Hannah's name, printed again at the bottom of the page, and also to the writing on the left side of the page, which appeared to move in a different direction than the rest of the lines. The teacher explained that children Hannah's age often use space creatively, turning the paper to fill up empty margins when they run out of space at the bottom of a page. Hannah's mother confirmed that she had often seen

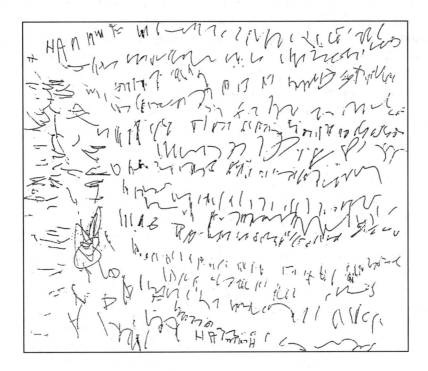

FIGURE 2.7. Hannah's second meeting notes.

Hannah turning a paper around and around as she wrote, and both women agreed that Hannah must have had a long meeting!

The pleasurable, collaborative sharing of stories about Hannah's writing exemplifies the type of interaction between home and school that both acknowledges the importance of parents' observations and offers them additional insight into their children's development. This teacher chose to set up a "Parents' Corner"—a bulletin board just inside the door—on which she posted copies of notes to be sent home, pages for parents to sign up to help in the classroom or to chaperone outings, and space for parents to post pictures and artifacts from home to share with children, teachers, and other parents. Typical photographs included children reading favorite storybooks, attempting to spell familiar words with magnetic letters on the refrigerator, or playing with alphabet puzzles. When writing samples were brought in, the teacher summarized the parent's story of the writing and displayed the explanation along with the writing sample and photo.

This process allowed the teacher to capture a picture of the children's home literacy and demonstrated the importance of all forms of writing and word play to everyone who perused the board. Samples brought in by some parents also probably encouraged other parents to watch for similar efforts at home and to help them notice more about the ways that preschoolers experiment with print and writing. The desire to see their own children represented on the board might even have prompted some parents to provide their children with writing and print materials and to join in children's efforts with them.

Establishing comfortable routines for sharing stories of literacy development also can help parents and other caregivers feel comfortable enough with the teacher to discuss any concerns they may have about their child's emerging literacy. Parents occasionally are worried about backward letters or other errors, such as in directionality. These concerns sometimes cause parents to worry that their children might have a learning disability. Teachers can assure parents that letter reversals and inconsistent directionality are perfectly normal during the preschool years, and, in fact, persist for many letters well into first and second grades.

The coloring book pages shown in Figure 2.8 might cause concern had Daniel's mother not been aware of the normal course of writing development. Four-year-old Daniel colored the page at the top (Figure 2.8a) by himself at home and then wrote his name on the bottom from right to left, reversing most of the letters. At his request, his aunt colored the page on the bottom. When both had finished coloring, Daniel proclaimed that his aunt's coloring was better and promptly signed his name to that picture, too, this time writing it from left to right (Figure 2.8b). When his teacher saw this sample and heard the story about its production, she was able to point out that Daniel was probably using solid logic to determine how to write his name in the coloring book. His rule was to start from the center binding, not from the left, and work out from there. His teacher also marveled at Daniel's ability to flip the letters around spatially to write them. Few adults have that skill!

FIGURE 2.8. Daniel's name writing in a coloring book.

Daniel's mom laughed as she described Daniel taking credit for his aunt's coloring, and the teacher noted that Daniel seemed to understand the power that writing his name has. The teacher's note about this brief sharing included the fact that Daniel was coloring with his aunt, a sign that the extended family was involved in his literacy development. She was sure to post this sample in the Parents' Corner, knowing that it would provide some reassurance to other parents about the common use of backward writing by preschoolers.

As noted, the Parents' Corner also allowed parents or other primary caregivers to post pictures of the children engaged in activities at home or on family outings. Photographs of special events, such as a new brother's bris or a Japanese child's celebration of Children's Day with his siblings, prompted both parents and children to share personal stories. Children were encouraged to tell about the people in the pictures and what was happening, a kind of oral composition that we discuss in detail in a later chapter. The teacher also encouraged parents to bring in pictures of the ordinary days in children's lives to affirm the value of everyday family interaction.

Most parents now have phones with built-in cameras and are accustomed to photographing their children. Many parents routinely texted pictures to the teacher with their explanations in the form of brief text messages. Recognizing that not all families had the financial resources to take and send photographs, however, the teacher also obtained an easy-to-operate digital camera through a donation and sent it home each week with a different family. She asked parents to try to "catch" their children reading and writing. For those using the borrowed camera, the teacher set aside time when it was returned to download and discuss pictures, and to print some for posting in the Parent's Corner.

Figure 2.9, a photo brought in by Emily's mother, shows Emily and her classmate, Stephanie, absorbed with their writing, working amid a variety of paints, paper, and markers on the kitchen table. Figure 2.10 is the writing sample that Emily's mother sent in to accompany the picture. When she spoke with the teacher later, she described how Emily and Stephanie both contributed to the sample, alternately drawing and writing using a variety of scribbles, pretend letters, a signature, and other actual letters. This sample provided yet another chance for the teacher to demonstrate that all of these forms of writing were valued. Its placement on the board prompted other parents to bring in similar samples that they recognized as significant after seeing the bulletin board display.

When teachers and parents begin to collaborate about literacy development early on in children's lives, many parents carry forward an expectation for involvement as their children progress through school. These expectations encourage parents to advocate for their children and to remain involved in their learning. Hannah's parents demonstrated this when Hannah turned 4 and moved to a new preschool class. Assuming that the new teacher would also want to share observations about Hannah's writing, the child's mother brought in the sample in Figure 2.11 without waiting for the teacher to ask. The teacher happily discussed the

FIGURE 2.9. Stephanie and Emily drawing and writing at home.

sample with her and learned that Hannah and her dad had written it together, at Hannah's request. At this point, Hannah was aware that writing is done with letters; she spent lots of time, both at home and at school, practicing writing letters. She also knew that words have correct spellings and often asked adults to spell words she wanted to write. Hannah's mother reported that her husband provided all the conventional spellings evident in this piece, while Hannah wrote some words herself, with no effort to map sounds to letters.

FIGURE 2.10. Emily and Stephanie's joint writing.

FIGURE 2.11. Hannah's writing with her dad.

Examining this writing sample with Hannah's parents allowed her teacher to see that Hannah's literacy efforts were well supported at home. Adding a copy of this sample and a summary of her conversation with Hannah's mother to the child's writing folder provided valuable assessment information. As the folder was filled with additional samples from both home and school over the course of the school year, a clear picture of Hannah's progress emerged.

Challenges to Collaboration

Teachers who involve parents in observing, documenting, and sharing their preschoolers' experimentation with print must be prepared for a number of challenges. They must recognize how differences in culture, family composition, literacy levels, language, and beliefs about how children become literate affect how parents and caregivers interact with teachers (Lilly & Green, 2004). Teachers need to examine carefully their own assumptions about parents' and caregivers' roles in their children's education and make sure that they keep an open mind as they hear family stories and find strengths in what is shared (Kieff & Wellhousen, 2000). This is especially true if the behaviors described don't fit the teacher's own experiences and beliefs about home literacy environments.

Daniel's teacher, for example, frowns on coloring books, preferring open-ended art activities. When Daniel's mother brought in the coloring book pages in Figure 2.8, his teacher could have used the opportunity to suggest that encouraging the child to color on blank paper might be better. But doing so would have ignored the fact that the child engaged in a valid and valuable interaction with his aunt as part of the coloring book activity. The teacher's choice not to include coloring books in her own classroom, though wise, does not negate the fact that in many homes, these books offer opportunities for wonderful interaction between parents and children.

Teachers might also discover that parents' views about getting children ready for kindergarten involve some unrealistic expectations about literacy development. For example, some parents worry that their children aren't developing at a proper rate, and they sometimes ask teachers to engage children in activities that are not appropriate. Later chapters in this book provide a guide to the typical progression of print understanding and writing in young children. Teachers can share this information with parents to help them understand and support their children's literacy development.

The Promise of Home–School Partnerships

Collaboration with parents requires work, but the results are worth the effort. All parents can offer insight into how their children engage with print outside the classroom. Bringing parents into frequent conversations about their children, and sharing the joys and concerns embedded in their stories, can unite teachers and families in their resolve to do what is best for individual children. These exchanges also provide opportunities for teachers and parents to develop an appreciation for each other's perspectives on children's learning. This exchange sometimes leads families to bring more of the literacy interactions that occur at school into their homes. Equally important, exchanges with families also help teachers to provide opportunities and interactions in the preschool that match those with which children are comfortable at home. In either case, the happy result may be both home and school contexts that support children's emerging literacy.

Myths about Preschool Literacy Environments

Teachers must complete their daily morning message before children arrive. It is best to keep it the same every day so children can read it easily while the teacher points to the words.

While a morning message routine can be an effective way to help children make the connection between oral language and print, we have seen far too many classrooms where this practice has become an empty routine, with children parroting back memorized messages in singsong voices with little attention to the actual print. The routine will be more effective if children participate in creating the message. While the teacher may prepare the beginning of the message before children arrive, writing, for example, "Good morning! Today is . . . ," it is best if the remainder of the message is tied to calendar routines and events of the day. Thus children will be much more engaged as they watch while the teacher writes the date and a simple statement of what the children will be doing that day. They may also contribute their own ideas. Depending on the children's abilities, they may be able to chime in with suggested letters as the teacher spells out words. Then the completed message can be read in unison while the teacher points to each word. This simple change often results in children revisiting the message during free-choice center time to practice reading on their own.

There can never be too much print in a preschool classroom.

It is generally true that a lot of print in the classroom environment is a good thing. Yet we need to be aware of visual clutter! At some point, too much print becomes the visual equivalent of white noise—always in the background and no longer noticed. Environmental print is most effective when it is useful. While simple labels on some items might entice children to attend to print, as we saw with Keviana's attempt to read the word *refrigerator* in her classroom's housekeeping center, labeling everything in a classroom serves little useful purpose. Children are more likely to attend to print that is meaningful to them. Their own names that show where to store their belongings or display their individual work, or labels on storage bins that help children put materials away when they finish with them are much more likely to engage their interest!

Preschool children are too young to use technology. They need to be shielded from "screen time" when they are at school.

There is validity to concerns about the amount of time children spend in front of electronic screens, whether watching television, playing on a computer, or using a smartphone, iPad, or video game. Despite dire warnings about the negative effects of technology on children, as seen in social media postings almost daily, there is actually surprisingly little solid research on the effects of specific types of interactive technology use on children's learning and development. Many earlier studies about negative impacts were based on children's use of passive technology, as with TV viewing. There is no avoiding the fact that children in preschool today are "digital natives" born into a world filled with technology that they use all the time and that they will be expected to have mastery over as early as primary grades where they will encounter standardized assessments that are administered exclusively on computers or electronic tablets. While this prospect frightens many adults, children who have played with their parents' smartphones since they were toddlers find this to be quite natural. The tenets of Developmentally Appropriate Practice (NAEYC, 2009) include providing learning opportunities that are appropriate relative to children's culture and social environment. Denying children meaningful, high-quality experiences to explore the world of electronic print has the potential to cut them off from an important part of mainstream culture.

The most important consideration is what screen time replaces in a child's daily routine. Technology offers what to many children will be more engaging and appealing interaction with print than traditional paper-and-pencil classroom activities. Substituting iPad print manipulation apps for activities that have children sitting quietly copying letters or sorting word cards swaps one sedentary, symbolic activity with another. Teachers just need to ensure that screen time does not displace more hands-on, active learning opportunities through which children manipulate and explore real, rather than digital, items in their environments. Nor should digital play overtake opportunities for construction or dramatic and rough-and-tumble social play. The key to effective use of technology is in selecting high-quality interactive learning apps and computer programs and balancing the time children engage in quiet, digital exploration with active, socially engaging play. For extensive discussion of technology and young children, see the joint statement from NAEYC and the Fred Rogers Center for Early Learning and Children's Media (2012) at *www.naeyc.org/content/technology-and-young-children*.

IDEAS FOR DISCUSSION, REFLECTION, AND ACTION

1. Share your daily planning structure with others. Is there a plan for incorporating technology into daily activity? Is time for whole-group, small-group, and one-on-one instruction built in? What can you learn from others about dealing with the challenges of differentiated instruction?

2. Consider the picture in Figure 2.12. Given the guidelines for print-rich classroom environments in this chapter, critique the space depicted. What are the strengths and drawbacks of this area of the classroom? What changes might you make to enhance the possibility that children will learn about print from this environment?

3. To promote a more effective discussion of the classroom environment, plan a series of visits to various classrooms. Invite host teachers to lead a tour of what is observed in the environment, including how it evolved and is used. Share ideas for enriching the environment and effectively using materials.

4. Identify a theme for a dramatic play center to complement each unit in your preschool curriculum. With other preschool teachers using the same curriculum, use the planning guide in Table 2.2 to determine what materials will enhance children's experimentation with print in each center.

FIGURE 2.12. Preschool print environment.

CHAPTER 3

Connecting Oral Language to Print Knowledge

Daniel approached his preschool teacher, Mrs. Levy, with a picture he had just drawn. "I know a lot about dinosaurs," he said. "Can you write my story for me?" He then dictated as Mrs. Levy wrote on a piece of note-paper: "This is Tyrannosaurus Rex. He is as tall as a telephone pole. He's a meat eater. He eats lots of other dinosaurs. His tooth is six inches. They died. They got buried and the mud turned into rock and sometimes you can find a footprint as long as your arm." When she handed him the dic-tated message, he was impressed with the amount of print. He promptly went to the art table to tape the writing to the bottom of his drawing, then stowed his creation in his cubby. When his mother arrived to pick him up at the end of the day, he exclaimed, "Look what I wrote!"

A conventional view of literacy would suggest that Daniel was stretching the truth, perhaps exuberantly taking credit for the writing his teacher produced. In recent years, though, the definition of literacy has expanded to recognize multiple forms of communication. The term "literacies" (Larson, 2006) is used to encom-pass all acts of meaning making, whether attending to print to comprehend a message or extracting messages from illustrations or videos; whether using print to write traditional compositions or sharing meaning through photographs, songs, or video. Regardless of the form, oral language is foundational to all aspects of literacy development.

If we consider multiple literacies, Daniel certainly engaged in literate actions as he drew a dinosaur picture and shared information about dinosaurs verbally with his teacher. The source of Daniel's information about Tyrannosaurus Rex was picture books about dinosaurs in his classroom as well as documentary videos he watched avidly at home. That Daniel could listen to these books read aloud, examine pictures in the books, and attend to videos to learn dinosaur facts from all three sources further illustrates his engagement in meaning making. Since Daniel was not yet able to read print as a source of information, he had to rely on the oral language surrounding his investigation of all things dinosaur. This chapter will address the connections among oral language, reading, and writing, as well as strategies to encourage and support meaning making in the preschool classroom.

CONNECTIONS BETWEEN ORAL LANGUAGE AND READING

While the focus of this book is how children learn about print for reading and writing, we must again stress that oral language, reading, and writing are all interrelated. Print is meaningless unless children connect it to language they know. The extent to which children's language ability, and especially their vocabulary, impacts reading development has been well documented (Biemiller, 2006; Hart & Risley, 2003; NELP, 2009). The more words children know, the more they will eventually be able to read. And the more children read, the more new words they learn. Thus, children who begin with more language ability and larger vocabularies have increased capacity for continuing to build both language and reading skills as compared to children who begin formal schooling with less-well-developed language. In fact, comprehension difficulties among children as late as fifth grade have been shown to connect to early language difficulties (Justice, Mashburn, & Petscher, 2013).

The connection between oral language and the development of print knowledge may be less readily apparent. Beyond promoting development of extensive oral language vocabularies that will enable children to attach meaning to the print they encounter, immersion in rich oral language environments also helps children develop a more fundamental type of knowledge. That is, they develop knowledge of how language sounds and how it is used to communicate meaning.

Oral language is related to learning the sounds of language because the more children speak and are spoken to, the more variety of words they hear. This includes hearing words that sound very similar, yet have completely different meanings, often due to very small changes in the phonemes within words. Consider the confusion of one preschool child who was convinced that the first of the Billy Goats Gruff was injured after crossing the bridge and bleating to his siblings that they should follow. Upon questioning the child, her teacher realized that she had confused the words *bleating* and *bleeding*—a difference of one phoneme in the middle of the word. The teacher reread the sentence from the book, emphasizing the word *bleating*, and then wrote it and the word *bleeding* on a chart so the children could compare how each word looked and notice how the /d/ and /t/ sounds were represented. In this way, the children learned both new vocabulary and gleaned information about how print is related to sound.

That children do hear and attend to parts of words in oral language to construct meaning was evident in the following exchange as a 4-year-old attempted to express what she was thinking after her teacher finished reading *Rabbits and Raindrops* (Arnosky, 2001a) to the class.

> MRS. GAINES: Who can tell me something the rabbits did when it started to rain? Yes, Jasmine?
>
> JASMINE: They rolled up in their . . . their package.
>
> MATTHEW: There's no package in this story!
>
> MRS. GAINES: I know Jasmine knows what she's talking about. Let's let her explain.
>
> JASMINE: They rolled under. . . . , under, like, the bushes.
>
> MRS. GAINES: Oh! That's right. They went under the bushes. The author said "hedges." That's a word for a row of bushes growing together. Hedge. It does sound like "package" at the end. This is how we write the word *package*. (demonstrates on the bottom of the chart the group is creating together.) And this is how we write *hedge*. See? They both end with *ge*. This word from the book is *hedge*. Good listening, Jasmine!

This exchange suggests that even when teachers do not intentionally focus preschoolers' attention on the sounds of language, children absorb what they hear and sometimes actively apply what they know about language—even knowledge of phonemes within words—to construct meaning.

CONNECTIONS BETWEEN ORAL LANGUAGE AND COMPOSITION

While it is clear that children rely on oral language when they read, that is also the case when they write. One of the most important things to understand about preschool children's writing is that it does rest on oral language. Children first learn to compose through talk—when they tell stories about events in their lives at home, retell stories from favorite books or television shows, act out story lines in their dramatic play, explain their drawings or paintings, or talk about something of interest in the classroom. When Roberto tells his classmates about the hedgehog he encountered in the petting zoo, he is likely to be asked, "Did you pet it? What did it feel like? Did it stick you? How big was it? What did it eat?" As Roberto responds, he learns to extend his explanations to include more information. He also learns to consider what his audience—in this case, his classmates and teacher—want to know. Roberto and his classmates are socialized into thinking through what they say during shared interactions. The skills that children develop through these kinds of oral language interactions are exactly those they need if they are to grow as writers.

In fact, a multiple literacies view would suggest that many forms of oral language are, in fact, forms of authoring. Authoring encompasses the many ways that children create meaning, including through oral compositions such as the one Daniel composed to tell about dinosaurs. It also includes the talk that occurs in dramatic play as children engage in dialogue in the voices of the characters they create (Hall & Robinson, 2003; Mendoza & Kats, 2008), and in conversations when they tell stories about their experiences. Simmerman and colleagues (2012) contended that "in order to survive and thrive, young people must become proficient in their ability to think clearly and express their thinking" (p. 293). Authoring is a way that preschool children express their thinking, whether through gestures, play, drawing, composing messages orally, or attempting to write their own messages.

Children who are drawn into talk in preschool classrooms begin to internalize the many functions that oral language serves. For example, they learn to use language to name, label, and describe things and events. They also learn to use language to make their needs known, to request help, and to persuade others to join them in play. Once engaged in play, they use language to create scenarios and to direct play actions. All of these functions of language can also be accomplished later through writing.

The more varied are young children's uses of oral language, the more varied will be their later uses of written language. A child who has learned to speak up to ask classmates to leave his block structure standing will eventually recognize that he can make a sign that says, "Don't knock this down!" A child who wants to tell everyone all about her pet tarantula will discover that she can draw a picture and compose a message about the tarantula to share. What children learn to do with oral language, they may also choose to do in writing.

The types of writing in which preschool children engage are connected to their interests and to the kinds of classroom activities toward which they gravitate. Children who have creative interests tend to use writing materials to experiment with new literacy processes and new uses for those materials. Those with more conceptual interests use writing to explore and record their thoughts about topics they find interesting, as Daniel did when he addressed his interest in dinosaurs by dictating an oral composition to his teacher. Children who are more socially oriented use writing to mediate joint social interactions and further their play with peers. Still other children are more procedurally oriented and use writing materials to practice forms of writing, perhaps experimenting with pages of letters and letter-like forms without intending any particular meaning (Rowe & Neitzel, 2010).

These findings suggest that teachers have opportunities to support children's development of oral language, reading, and writing throughout the day and across many typical preschool activities and routines. Teachers do have a role to play in helping young children extend their language and eventually move from oral composition to graphic expressions of meaning, including writing, whether in child-directed play, teacher-directed activities, or conversations that occur as teachers and children interact in every area of the classroom.

Oral Composition and Writing in Dramatic Play

In dramatic play centers, children explore storytelling as they act out scenarios from their everyday lives or reenact stories they have heard from books. Equally important, they create fantasy scenarios in which story lines are developed and plots are carried forward by actions (Edwards, 1990; Kavanaugh & Engle, 1998; McCaslin, 1996; Mendoza & Katz, 2008). Teachers can extend the language of children's play by participating in it occasionally. One teacher, having observed that two children playing veterinarian in a dramatic play center were losing interest in their roles, brought over a stuffed dog and said, "My dog got hit by a car! Can you help?" The children promptly began examining the dog, giving each other directions for taking X-rays, bandaging a hurt paw, and prescribing medicine for the injured animal. One child even offered advice to the pet owner about preventing her dog from getting out of the yard. By joining in the children's play, the teacher extended both the duration of the children's pretense and the language used to sustain the play scenario.

As teachers interact with children to extend their oral language in dramatic play, they can also nudge children toward using writing props. For example, the teacher who took her dog to the vet responded to the children's verbal instructions by asking, "Can you write that down for me so I don't forget when I get home?" The veterinarian hastily scribbled on a notepad in the dramatic play center. Handing the note to the teacher, she read, "Change the bandage every day. Give him one pill with his food. Lock your gate." While the scribbles were not recognizable as an actual message, the child's reading of what she intended confirmed that she did, indeed, compose a purposeful message.

The teacher could also have asked the children for a receipt or to schedule a follow-up appointment. Such requests would help children experiment with specific functions of writing and also encourage them to include writing as an integral part of their pretend play (Casbergue, McGee, & Bedford, 2008; Christie, 1991; Kieff & Casbergue, 1999; Roskos & Neuman, 1993). Interactions like these are especially appropriate for children who are oriented toward social play.

As noted in Chapter 2, almost any play scenario can be enhanced to extend oral language and encourage interaction with print. Keep in mind, though, that the language children use while playing will almost certainly extend beyond their capacity for writing. Even when preschoolers wish to share their thoughts, few have the ability to engage in extended attempts to write conventionally using actual alphabet letters. Rather, children will use forms of emergent writing that range from drawing and scribbles to invented letter-like forms, strings of actual letters, and perhaps brief experimentation with early phonemic spelling. (Those different forms of writing are detailed in later chapters.) When children engage in oral composition or offer extended "readings" of their attempts to write, it is important to look beyond their primitive print and encourage their use of language to create meaning.

Authoring Informational Text

Just as teachers have a role in encouraging writing during play, it is also important for preschool teachers to foster children's ability to share what they are learning through informational (expository) composition. While some children may share information fairly easily, as did Daniel when he sought out a teacher to dictate what he knew about dinosaurs and fossils, many need encouragement.

Preschoolers are generally accustomed to talking about their immediate activities and surroundings. This type of talk is most often narrative in form. Informational composition, however, requires children to use a less familiar style of language. Expository texts encountered by preschool children are often used to describe characteristics of something, for example, and generally refer to attributes of a full class of objects. Thus, rather than referring to "Mrs. Spider" and detailing what she does as a character in a story, an informational text will describe attributes of spiders in general. A typical text might read, "Spiders have eight legs. Many spiders spin webs to catch insects for food."

Expository texts also contain specialized words for concepts that are often outside of children's everyday language. As children learn about new content, they will begin to understand related new vocabulary and use it in their oral compositions. When children's compositions begin to reference classes of objects, they demonstrate emerging awareness of written informational text. This awareness was evident when Daniel's stated that "*they* died" and "*they* got buried in the mud" rather than saying "*this* dinosaur died," referring explicitly to the one in his picture.

Expository composition that begins to approximate the language of informational text is best supported when children are provided with lots of topics to talk and write about, and when they hear lots of informational picture books read aloud to them. To engage children with interesting content, teachers can provide a well-equipped discovery center. Such a center contains objects for children to observe and handle (e.g., a pet canary in a cage, a bird nest, and some feathers), as well as informational picture books related to the objects. These books should be shared with the children during read-aloud sessions and also displayed in a way that invites children to explore them in the discovery center. It doesn't matter that the children can't read the books independently. Considerable information can be obtained and discussed as children examine the pictures and compare them to the artifacts in the discovery center. Figure 3.1 shows how simple and inviting such a display can be.

The information children derive from the artifacts and books in the classroom can be shared through both oral and written language. Inviting children to dictate pages to create "all about" books related to specific topics extends both oral language and children's recognition that what they say can be written down. These

FIGURE 3.1. Science discovery learning center.

activities will be most appealing to children who display conceptual interests. However, all children should be invited to participate so that they can develop the ability to think about, talk about, and eventually write about a variety of concepts.

In one preschool classroom, the 4-year-olds spent 3 weeks studying "creepy crawlies"—a focus of investigation that encompassed insects, arachnids, and reptiles, depending on children's interests. The discovery center contained an aquarium housing a tarantula on loan from one of the families; a Japanese cricket cage with a live cricket, also from a child's home; and a variety of insects mounted in magnifying boxes purchased from a teaching supply store. Children went on "bug hunts" in the play yard to find out where different creatures lived and to observe them in their natural habitats. They shared many books with their teachers about insects, spiders, worms, snakes, and centipedes. Periodically throughout this time of exploration, children were invited to draw pictures and dictate information about their favorite creatures for inclusion in a class book. As the following examples illustrate, children's contributions at the beginning of their investigation included simple statements or personalized narrations, possibly reflecting children's relative lack of knowledge about the topic, or perhaps initial lack of interest.

ERIC: Lizard. I like a lizard.

MAX: I like spiders. And I like spider webs too. I like spiders when they're on the spider webs.

GABRIELLA: Doodlebugs always roll up when you touch them. They always tickle when they are on your hand.

Many children included more information for dictations that were taken later in their investigation of creepy crawlies, suggesting that the more knowledge children gained, the more interested they became in the topic, and the more information they had to share. As the investigation continued, the teacher also engaged in more extended conversations with children about what they were learning and used those conversations to draw out more information as children dictated what they wanted to say about the pictures they drew. The increase in information can be seen in the following example.

TEACHER: Kate, what do you want me to write to go with your picture?

KATE: (*pointing to her picture of three snakes*) Snakes.

TEACHER: Is there anything else you want to write?

KATE: I like snakes.

TEACHER: I know you really like looking at our books about snakes. What snakes do you like best?

KATE: I like purple ones and rattlesnakes and milk snakes and coral snakes.

TEACHER: So you learned about some different kinds of snakes!

KATE: I learned rattlesnakes and coral snakes have poison that will make you dead, but milk snakes don't have poison.

TEACHER: That's great information for our book. Let's write that.

Thus, in response to brief discussion about her picture, Kate was able to express very specific knowledge that would not have been evident from either her picture or her first responses to her teacher's query about what should be written on her page of the class book. Similar conversations about the pictures children drew over the 3 weeks of the investigation resulted in even more detailed and mostly accurate dictations from Leo, Caitlin, and Tyrone as seen in the information they dictated with little prompting at the end of their study of creepy crawlies.

LEO: Ladybugs. They spit a yellow liquid so birds can't eat them. They eat bad bugs. They eat leaves. They're red and orange. They have a back with spots and red.

CAITLIN: Butterflies. They fly and they eat other bugs. And they eat plants. They lay their eggs on plants.

TYRONE: Ladybugs. I learned about not to mush them. To hold them careful. They live in the grass. They eat those green bugs.

From these dictated messages, it is evident that the children in this classroom gained significant information about the creatures that were the focus of their

investigation. It is also clear that their compositions were beginning to approximate informational text features as they discussed classes of animals (snakes,
doodlebugs, ladybugs) in the plural and in present tense, and as they incorporated
content-specific vocabulary like spider webs, poison, rattlesnake, and coral snake,
and content-specific concepts such as laying eggs on leaves and spitting yellow
liquid to avoid predators.

Composing in the Writing Center

In addition to teacher-directed activities aimed at fostering composition, children
frequently attempt to compose informational text and stories independently, especially when their classrooms contain a well-stocked writing center. While it is clear
from the preschoolers' dictations or readings of what they have written that some
children have a lot to say about topics in which they have an interest, it is also clear,
upon examination of their independent attempts, that their writing lags behind
their oral language. As noted earlier, this is typical. Just as babies can understand
many more words than they are able to say, so too can preschoolers construct oral
compositions that are more sophisticated than they can convey in writing.

The writing sample in Figure 3.2 is Christopher's attempt to write his own
page for the class book about insects using materials in the writing center. He read
it to his teacher as, "Spiders. Poison. Spiders live on rocks." Christopher indicated
that the objects on the left in his composition were rocks and spider webs, while
other lines were words intended to function as labels for objects in the picture and

FIGURE 3.2. Christopher's writing center composition.

a simple statement about spiders. While he had not yet developed a conventional understanding of writing, he was beginning to develop a good sense of how to convey information about a specific topic.

The gap between what children can write and their oral composition ability is equally evident in their narratives. Figure 3.3 represents 4-year-old Emily's story about a flower. The only conventional writing in this sample is her name. She asked her teacher to write down the story that went with her picture, signaling an understanding of the difference between drawing and writing. Emily's dictations revealed that she was developing into a competent storyteller.

"Once upon a time, there was a flower. It was snowing and it froze to death. It didn't have any water forever and ever. And then one day it did get some water because the person saw it wasn't going to get any water. And along came an ant that said, 'I'm going to eat you, flower.' But the ant was joking. And I hope you feel better flower because it's still freezing but it did get water. The flower felt better because it found a lake and thought it would be fun."

While the plot of her story is disjointed, it is clear that Emily understood that stories have conflict—in this case a flower freezing to death without water and being threatened by an ant—and that stories end when the conflict is resolved. While she didn't yet have the ability to write her story using print, she was nonetheless successful in composing it.

FIGURE 3.3. Emily's flower story.

Both Christopher and Emily's compositions were created in their classroom writing centers. With teachers' support and encouragement, they benefited from time and materials that enabled them to write independently, for their own purposes, using whatever form of writing they wished. While Emily's "writing" was composed entirely of pictures, with the exception of her name, Christopher included writing, in the form of scribbles placed beside his picture of rocks and spider webs. In both cases, the writing center offered the children the freedom to experiment with composition and forms of writing.

SUPPORTING ATTENTION TO THE LANGUAGE OF BOOKS

Both the narrative and information compositions described thus far suggest children's emerging awareness of the way written text sounds. In fact, young children's pretend readings of familiar storybooks have been shown to develop along a predictable path with the most sophisticated picture-driven attempts (those made before children begin to attend to the actual print) including nearly verbatim language from the texts (Sulzby, 1986).

Frequently hearing many different kinds of books read aloud may be sufficient for many children to begin to internalize the language of written text. Narrative text features may be the easiest for some children to recognize and reproduce in their compositions since they tend to reflect the natural storytelling language children use every day as they relate their own experience. The influence of books can be seen even in children's narratives, however, when conventions typical of written language creep into their stories. Consider the following excerpts from a You Tube video of a French preschooler's storytelling (Yelynn, 2012):

> "Winnie the Pooh and Tigger woke up and saw that the baby monkeys were gone. And then the baby monkeys were lost in the trees. They saw bats. They saw crocodiles, hippopotamus, and giraffes. They had taken a very long trip. . . . They saw boxes of animals who are poor who couldn't find their way."

Her story goes on to describe animals being jailed because they couldn't pay for their food, and daring battles with helmets, swords, shields, and magic powers used to defeat a witch defending her strawberries. The story, and her animated telling of it, is charming. The influence of many stories she has heard is evident in her choice of characters, including among others Winnie, Tigger, a witch, and a lion "who is the king." That influence is equally apparent in the written language forms she includes in her story. Phrases like "and saw that," "they had taken," and "animals who are poor" and "who couldn't find their way" do not typically occur in everyday natural language. Rather, they are the language of written stories—language adopted by this child in her oral composition.

Not all children will attend to and internalize the language of written texts so readily, however, and most will benefit from more direct instruction designed to draw their attention to how oral language is crafted into written text. One effective way to do this is to engage children in shared writing activities following the reading of both informational and narrative books. (Specific instructions for conducting shared writing lessons are found in Chapter 4.) Classwide group lessons in which preschool children are invited to respond to a book they have just heard read aloud (McGee, 2007) can be especially helpful. Consider how one teacher engaged her group of 4-year-olds in discussion and shared writing after reading aloud from an alphabet book about construction.

TEACHER: We learned about some new construction equipment that I don't think we have seen before. Let's write about some of the equipment. I'm going to write a title at the top of our page: "Construction Equipment" (*speaking slowly as she writes each word on chart paper while the children watch*). Now, what should we write first?

MICHAEL: Backhoe!

TEACHER: What does the backhoe do? Let's look at that page. (*Shows the children the picture of the backhoe.*)

MICHAEL: It digs up lots of dirt.

TEACHER: That's right. It says here, "The backhoe pushes into the earth and pulls back a pile of dirt and rock." So what should we write?

MICHAEL: A backhoe pulls up dirt.

Michael's teacher repeated each word as she wrote it on the chart. Through this brief interaction, Michael's teacher extended his initial utterance that simply named a piece of equipment to a full sentence describing its function. Notice that, in addition to eliciting a longer utterance, specific reference to the relevant page apparently enticed Michael to use more direct language from the book as he described the backhoe *pulling up* dirt, rather than just *digging*—a more precise description of how the construction machinery actually works.

She continued this process with four more children who volunteered names of construction equipment, returning to the pictures to invite children to express their own thoughts, confirming their information with the actual words from the text, and then asking the children to summarize again. After the children had added to the chart, often with others offering comments of their own, the teacher reread the entire chart, tracking the print with a pointer while the children followed along. She then ended the whole group activity with a promise that children could continue to add to the chart on their own during center time later in the morning.

In this way, a whole-group oral language and writing activity was extended into another routine part of the day (Casbergue et al., 2008) as children visited the easel with the alphabet book propped on its ledge to examine the book and make their own additions to the chart. Some attempted to copy words from the book, while others drew or wrote with random letters or scribbles. Figure 3.4 shows the chart midway through center time.

USING TECHNOLOGY TO FOSTER ORAL COMPOSITION

We have so far described a variety of ways that teachers can encourage oral composition and early writing as children play, as they use materials in writing centers, as they explore interesting content in discovery centers, as they dictate their ideas in many different contexts, and as they participate in shared reading and writing activities. Emerging technology for young children offers an additional avenue for encouraging oral composition.

A number of new apps for smartphones and tablets can be used with preschool children to encourage them to draw and write. In fact, teachers have reported that some children are highly motivated to draw and write using tablets (Shifflet, Toledo, & Mattoon, 2012).

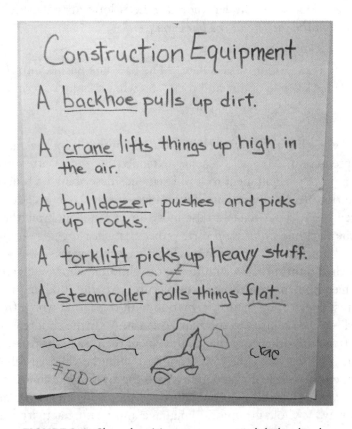

FIGURE 3.4. Shared writing responses to alphabet book.

Some of the best apps allow children to embed recordings of their own voices as they dictate text to accompany their pictures or read aloud their own writing attempts. Book Creator for iPad, by Red Jumper Limited, is one such app. Creating books with this program is simple. Children may draw and write on each page they want to create using a finger as a pen, or they can paste in pictures from image files stored on the device. They can even do both! Blank pages are nearly the full dimensions of the screen, making it easy for young children to work within the available space. If they shrink pictures slightly, a simple matter of using a finger to slide the edge of a picture, they gain white space to write captions or more extensive text. Once they are satisfied with their pages, they can activate a microphone that will let them record their own narration. When they do so, a speaker icon appears on the page. Children can tap that button to hear their own recordings each time they return to the book. With this app, it is possible to add multiple recordings to each page. This feature is especially beneficial for children who are English language learners, as recordings can be made in both English and a child's native language (Rowe & Miller, in press).

Figure 3.5 shows one page of a book entitled "My Family" created by 5-year-old Isabella. As part of a class project, her mother sent pictures of family members to the teacher who saved them on a classroom iPad. Bella selected a picture for each page of her book, wrote a caption, then recorded herself reading her captions. For this page, the initial recording said, "My baby brother." In addition to reading what they have written as Bella did, children can also be recorded as they tell more

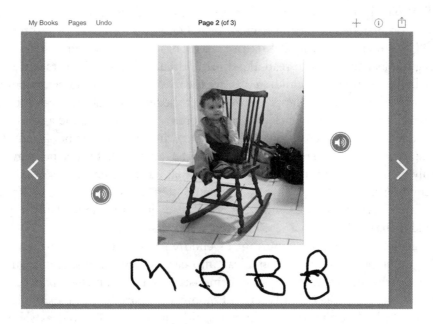

FIGURE 3.5. An e-book page for "My Family" book.

extended stories of what is happening in the picture. Bella returned to this page another day and added another recording. In it, she said, "My brother's name is Braden. He is almost 2. He climbed in this chair at my aunt's house all by himself."

There is a growing body of evidence that children as early as preschool can learn to use touch-screen devices very quickly and then begin to use them for their own exploration and creative pursuits (Couse & Chen, 2010). When that is the case, these technologies offer another avenue for encouraging oral and written composition in the preschool classroom.

SCAFFOLDING CHILDREN'S ATTENTION TO LANGUAGE

Whether engaging children in conversations in which they relate their experiences or extending their language as they participate in classroom activities, skillful teachers know that their most important role is to scaffold children's language use. "Scaffolding" refers to the process whereby a child's learning occurs in the context of full performance of a task as adults gradually relinquish support (Cazden, 1988). Adults frequently help children accomplish things they want to do, such as working with a puzzle, writing the first letters of their names, or riding bikes. First, we show them how we do the task. Then, we invite them to try and help as they attempt to do it. At times we intervene, but only when our assistance is needed. When we think they are ready, we let them try the task on their own, while observing the independent attempt to determine what further assistance is needed.

Scaffolded instruction in reading and writing offers teachers opportunities to focus on many early literacy concepts, including the language of written texts (Cabell, Tortorelli, & Gerde, 2013). An example of scaffolding occurs when teachers use Big Books and charts to read aloud to children. When children track the print as teachers read aloud, the children observe the reading process and begin to understand that print tracks oral language. Although the teacher is doing the reading, the children can follow along mentally as some words are pointed out and as they notice how the reader moves across and down the page and through the book from front to back. After one or two repeated readings of the same book, the teacher may occasionally pause and point to a particular word that has been repeated several times. The children share in the reading by "filling in" that word. If the book is left in the library corner, many children will attempt to "read" it on their own. Thus, a type of scaffolding has occurred in a very informal, relaxed manner.

Scaffolding is equally important as children first begin to write, especially as they attempt to organize their ideas into early compositions. A similar scaffolding process occurs when teachers demonstrate writing on chart paper as children observe. As in the "Construction Equipment" shared writing example, children watched while the teacher wrote the title, and then observed as she wrote sentences dictated by the children. Scaffolding occurred as she helped individual children shape their responses into full sentences with accurate information, often including specific conceptual knowledge from shared reading of an alphabet book. Finally, she encouraged children to reread the book and write on the class chart independently.

Scaffolding is also evident in the teacher's interaction with Kate as the child dictated a message to accompany her drawing of three snakes. When Kate's initial response consisted of only a single word label for her picture, her teacher persisted with additional questioning to help Kate share additional knowledge about different kinds of snakes, eventually resulting in a more fully developed oral composition for her page in a class book.

Scaffolding will be necessary as children begin using technology to create e-books with their own drawing and writing. While many young children now arrive for preschool already comfortable with touch-screen technology after playing with their parents' smartphones, their experience is more likely to be with game apps and the camera functions than with book creation. Following the steps of scaffolding—demonstrating, inviting children to participate, and allowing independent practice with the new technology—will enhance the potential for children to use it in meaningful ways.

Successful scaffolding is always responsive to children's need for assistance and contingent on their responses to the help that is offered. Throughout this chapter, we have provided models of interactions between teachers and children in a variety of classroom contexts that enabled children to express their thoughts. Support for oral language provided a foundation for children to build their authoring skills—well in advance of their eventual development of traditional reading and writing skills.

A Myth about Supporting Oral Language in Preschool

Teachers should not interfere when children are playing in centers. Preschoolers need down time when they can just be children.

Children absolutely need time for free play during the day. It is also true, though, that they often seek out their teachers as playmates! Children are frequently drawn to centers where teachers are participating, and wise teachers are sure to circulate through all areas of the classroom to interact with as many children as possible.

More important, free play periods are ideal for engaging children in genuine conversations and responding to their individual interests. The Classroom Assessment Scoring System (CLASS; Pianta, LaParo, & Hamre, 2008) is now widely used to measure the quality of preschool classrooms, and is in fact required for all federally funded preschool programs. The instrument has been adopted because of its strong research base that links the teacher and classroom characteristics measured to children's later academic achievement.

One domain of behaviors assessed with this instrument is Instructional Support. This domain assesses teachers' ability to help children develop new concepts, model language, and provide high-quality feedback in their interactions with children. Specific indicators include scaffolding of children's thinking and language, helping children integrate new concepts with those previously learned, and helping them make connections between what they are learning and what they know from real-world experiences. The indicators also include frequent conversations, repetition and extension of children's language, and modeling of advanced language.

Nationwide, preschool classrooms receive the lowest scores for behaviors in this domain, in part because teachers do not demonstrate enough high-quality verbal interactions that are directly responsive to what children have to say (Justice, Mashburn, Hamre, & Pianta, 2009; LoCasale-Crouch et al., 2007). Yet teachers can learn to increase their responsiveness to children in ways that lead to children's engagement in extended conversational interactions (Cabell et al., 2011). Increases in the time teachers spend talking with children and improvement in their verbal interactions so that teachers are more intentional in their efforts to extend and support children's language and concept development have been shown to lead to both higher CLASS scores for preschool classrooms (Casbergue, Bedford, & Burstein, 2014) and enhanced vocabulary and early literacy development in preschool children (Casbergue, Burstein, & Bedford, 2014). Clearly, both children and teachers can benefit when teachers join in children's play.

IDEAS FOR DISCUSSION, REFLECTION, AND ACTION

1. Ask yourself, "Do I model, demonstrate, and guide practice to show students how to do something, rather than simply tell them to do it?"

2. Reflect on a typical day in your classroom. Is there a deliberate attempt to meet individual needs through personalized time with children? (Keep in mind that a pair of children constitutes a small group at the preschool level.) Are there some children who dominate the time you have for one-on-one conversation and instruction? Remember that all children need individual attention, but some may appear very independent or may be too shy to call attention to themselves. Consider how you might identify those children and plan to engage them in conversations.

3. Join with other preschool teachers who follow the same curriculum as you. For each theme or unit in the curriculum, plan a discovery center that will allow children to explore related concepts. For example, for a unit on light, shadows, and reflections, a discovery center might contain flashlights, mirrors, prisms, and collections of objects with reflective and matte surfaces. If there is sufficient space, the objects might be placed inside a small popup tent from within which children can project shadows onto the tent surface while others watch from outside. Remember that the materials should be inviting and draw children into the center. Be creative! Then prepare to spend lots of time there talking with the children.

4. Identify both narrative and expository picture books that can prompt extended discussion. For narrative texts, seek out books in which characters tackle complex problems and for which alternative actions are possible. For expository texts, seek out books with interesting new information and large detailed photographs that prompt children to see the environment in new ways. For each book, plan topics for shared writing that can follow read-aloud sessions.

CHAPTER 4

Developing Print and Alphabetic Knowledge for Reading

During center time in Ms. Swan's preschool classroom, three 4-year-olds were gathered in front of the easel that contained that day's morning message. Miriam glided a pointer from left to right under the lines of print as she "read" aloud, "Good morning, boys and girls. Today is Tuesday. We will have a fun day. The fireman is coming. We will have fun." She paused as she finished what she remembered of the message, realizing that there was still one more line of print. Undaunted, she continued her reading. "And we will have more fun." Of course, those were not the actual words on the chart, but her reading did contain the standard opening for this classroom's morning message. It was also true that the class was expecting a visit from a fireman, and the message stated that the visit would be fun.

Taking the pointer from her, André said, "I can find *fireman*. It starts with an *f*—f . . . f . . . f . . . fireman!" He correctly placed the pointer under the word *fireman*, but then also pointed to the word *fun*, stating, "And this word is *fireman*." Nicholas, who had watched both children, picked up a marker and said, "I can find the *F*'s!" He then drew a circle around each letter *F* on the chart.

In Chapter 3, we introduced the idea of using morning message and shared writing routines to encourage children's oral composition, both in teacher-directed activities and during free play in centers. Miriam, André, and Nicholas's use of the chart during their center time illustrates another perhaps more common use of materials designed for shared reading or created during shared writing: experimenting with print.

As noted in Chapter 1, the term *concepts of print* refers to knowledge of the functions of print and how print language works. This knowledge requires an understanding of the following:

- The overall structure of books and conventions of the printed word.
- The fact that print evokes meaning and has a variety of uses in people's lives.
- The notion that to make sense of print one needs to understand its directionality (i.e., front to back, top to bottom, and beginning to end).
- The concept of word (i.e., word boundaries and the visual order of letters within a word).
- The concept of letter (i.e., letters have distinct shapes, have names, and form words).

In addition to understanding concepts about print, children also need to develop an understanding of how print is used to represent oral language. It is not enough for children to be able to name all of the letters of the alphabet if they are to become readers. They must also come to recognize that the letters they know represent the sounds that they hear in spoken language. It is this connection of letters through sounds and then to word meanings that will ultimately enable children to read even words they do not recognize on sight.

The ability to make connections between the sounds of spoken language and print is contingent on children's development of phonemic awareness. As described in Chapter 1, phonemic awareness is the ability to hear, identify, and manipulate the individual sounds (phonemes) in spoken words. It is one aspect or type of phonological awareness, the understanding that words are made up of speech sounds, or phonemes. Activities that boost phonemic awareness build on broad aspects of phonological awareness, such as identifying and making oral rhymes and clapping out syllables in spoken words. However, phonemic awareness requires narrower and more advanced skills than rhyming and clapping syllables, and it links more directly to phonics, which relates sounds to the letters that represent them. Indeed, instruction in phonemic awareness, while focusing on the sounds heard in spoken words, may also involve the use of print.

The three children playing with their classroom morning message demonstrated understanding of many of these concepts. Miriam and André both overtly indicated knowledge of the connection between meaning and print, Miriam through her attempt to read the entire message, and André through his attempt to find specific words. Miriam also demonstrated conventional directionality in that she knew print was to be read from left to right and top to bottom. Because she swept the pointer under lines of print instead of pointing to individual words as she read, however, it is not as clear that she understood the concept of word. André, on the other hand, indicated that he was looking for a specific word and he was able to focus on two words within the lines of print, illustrating his understanding of the concept of word—even though he could not actually read both words correctly. Both André and Nicholas also demonstrated their understanding of the concept of letter. Nicholas used knowledge of letters to find and circle the *F*'s within words on the chart, indicating through both his words and his actions that he understood that words are comprised of individual letters. André used his knowledge of the same letter and of its corresponding sound to locate words he believed spelled *fireman*. In doing so, he also demonstrated the phonemic awareness skill of isolating a single sound within a word, as well as the ability to match sound to print.

Given the sustained attention these children were able to devote independently to the morning message, it is evident that they had been given many opportunities to learn about print. This chapter presents strategies that support children's development of concepts about print and the beginnings of alphabetic knowledge that is used for reading. Two overarching strategies presented here, shared reading and name games, are integrated instructional strategies. That is, they address many concepts of print within a broad activity framework. These strategies are intended to be used throughout the year to encourage children to use the print knowledge they are learning through more systematic, explicit teaching of alphabet letters and conceptual alphabetic knowledge.

Our overview of each of these strategies is followed by narrower activities that focus more specifically on a single print concept. These focused strategies concentrate on specific aspects of phonemic awareness, concepts about print, or alphabetic knowledge and may be used as follow up to whole-class instruction with small groups of children who need additional support. They may also be used for review with the whole class, if needed.

SHARED READING: AN INTEGRATED INSTRUCTIONAL STRATEGY

Shared reading involves activities in which the teacher reads aloud to children from materials that allow the children to see the print during the read-aloud. In preschool, the materials are generally Big Books or charts. As high-quality children's literature becomes more readily available in e-book format, teachers are also beginning to make use of smart boards that enable children to follow print as books are read aloud.

During shared reading, the teacher models the reading process as children observe or participate and respond. Shared reading has been shown to impact children's early language and literacy, especially vocabulary (NELP, 2008; Sénéchal, Pagan, Lever, & Ouellette, 2008). Here we focus on the manner in which the strategy can be used to call attention to print. Children whose teachers explicitly reference print during shared reading have been shown to make significant gains on standardized measures of both print knowledge and alphabet knowledge (Justice, Kaderavek, Fan, Sofka, & Hunt, 2011).

What Shared Reading Does

Books for young children that are rich in rhyming and alliteration are ideal for beginning phonological awareness activities. Many are available as Big Books, designed for reading in a group setting, where children can see the written words that represent speech. Shared reading with Big Books provides an excellent means of supporting children's knowledge about print and offers an informal bridge from phonological awareness to phonemic awareness and understanding of print.

In the following strategy, Big Books are used effectively in a whole–part–whole framework (Strickland, 1998) that allows children to experience a whole text before they look at the parts for explicit study. It also allows children to develop a context for using the skills they are learning. Rather than teaching skills in isolation, the whole–part–whole strategy introduces skills in combination with the strategies that utilize them.

There is no doubt that purely oral phonological awareness activities are foundational for reading and writing. However, activities that involve print can also be introduced, providing a playful, yet effective, way for children to simultaneously hear speech patterns and see how they are represented. This integrated strategy demonstrates how the instructional use of Big Books can extend beyond modeling the reading process. Repeated readings provide opportunities for children to listen to fluent reading, learn the language of print, and memorize text. Memorizing text leads children to "read" independently and begin to ask questions about the words on the page.

How to Do Shared Reading

Shared reading is most effective when teachers are intentional in their use of the strategy. The following series of steps from planning to engaging children in exploration of print will increase the likelihood that the strategy will lead to increases in children's knowledge of print for reading.

Step 1: Prepare for the Reading

Prepare by reading the Big Book to yourself, preferably several times, before sharing it with the children. Note aspects of the book that provide teaching opportunities, such as alliteration, repeated words, or phrases that enable children to "share" in the reading or match the text with word or phrase strips. Construct a mental and written plan for how you might use it to help children learn about print. You might attach sticky notes to specific pages to remind yourself of prospective teaching points.

Step 2: Introduce the Book

Start the first read-aloud by reading the title (while underlining it with your finger) and the names of the author and illustrator. If the cover provides clues about the story, ask a question such as "Now that you know the title and you can see the cover, what do you think this book might be about?" This question helps children learn to make predictions. Accept two or three responses. Always ask, "What made you think so?" This question requires children to give an explanation for their answers and discourages random guessing. It is an informal way of introducing young children to the idea that their responses should make sense. It also begins to introduce children to the idea of text-dependent close reading by suggesting that responses to books should be grounded in the material itself, a type of response reflected in newer standards for literacy, including the CCSS.

Step 3: Read the Book Aloud

Hold the book with the text facing the children so that they have a full view, as illustrated in Figure 4.1 Avoid tracking the print with your hands or a pointer, particularly during the first reading. Pointing too soon interferes with the children's ability to see the illustrations, which are integral to the text. It may also spoil the phrasing of the language in the book.

Step 4: Focus on Comprehension and Interpretation

Through skillful questioning, focus first on comprehension and interpretation. For example, consider a sample lesson using *I Went Walking* (Williams, 1989). This book lends itself to prediction questions throughout because the illustrator gives

FIGURE 4.1. Technique for shared reading.

visual clues about the story's events. The children can use these clues to guess what will happen next and then confirm their predictions as the next page is revealed. The book has a patterned text with two lines that are repeated throughout. For *I Went Walking*, the logical comprehension focus would be *making predictions*.

Step 5: Engage Children in Varied Responses

The second and third readings of the text should involve the children in multiple forms of response, such as drama or shared writing. The first reading involved oral language response focused on comprehension. Each subsequent reading should start with a full reading of the text followed by some form of response. *I Went Walking* is very simple: the main character goes walking, and each animal in the book joins him one at a time. Because the story has a repetitive quality and involves a number of animals, you might select a few children to act out the text as you read it aloud. Assign each child an animal character and one child as the main character. As you read the story, have the children listen for the names of their animals and join the others in marching around the room. Provide help as needed.

Step 6: Explore Print Features

After the children have gained familiarity with the book, you may wish to explore some of its print features during subsequent readings. Pace the activities according to the children's responses, and remember that this process should take place over time (perhaps 2 to 4 weeks), interspersed with a variety of other read-aloud books, charts, and Big Books.

The following list offers suggestions for explaining print features through matching sentences, words, and letters, respectively.

Matching Sentences. Remind children that several times during the past few weeks you have enjoyed this book with them. Today they are going to do something very special. On a piece of card stock, write two sentences or phrases from the book that are repeated often. Read them aloud to the children. Open the book to a page where one of the sentences or phrases is written. Ask the children to choose the phrase or sentence that matches the one in the book. Keep in mind that the children are not asked to read the sentence or phrase. They are simply matching it visually. Also remember that this may be challenging for some children. Give plenty of support. Point out the length of the phrase or sentence, the way it looks at the beginning and end, the spaces between words, and so on. The objective is to help children notice print more closely than they might have before.

Matching Words. As the children watch, cut one of the sentences or phrases matched above into its individual words. Have the children look at the sentence or phrase in the book and reconstruct it.

Matching Letters. Choose words that look and sound alike at the beginning, write them on cards, and have children find them in the book. Be sure that you read aloud the word on the card as you present it. For example, in *I Went Walking*, the words *went*, *walking*, and *what* are repeated many times. Once the children visually match the words on the cards to those in the book, read the words again, stressing the initial sound and noting how they look and sound alike at the beginning. Also, point out that all start with the letter *w*.

In summary, teachers support children's development of print concepts during shared reading when they:

- Select texts that lend themselves to repetition of phrases, sentences, and sound–symbol relationships.
- Allow for a variety of types of response to the same text, including discussion, drama, and shared writing.
- Allow for multiple ways to explore the features of print, such as visually matching sentences, words, and letters and reconstructing sentences and words.
- Support connections of phonemic awareness to print (e.g., rhyming and alliteration).
- Model directionality (left to right, return sweep, and top to bottom).
- Encourage the use of the language of literacy (e.g., *book*, *beginning/end of story*, *page*, *top/bottom of page*, *letter*, *word*, and *sentence*).

Variation

Sharing Poetry

Teachers often share poetry and song charts with children. Young children are frequently able to memorize the words after several weeks of verbal practice. Use these materials and point to the words as they are "read" or sung. Once children are very familiar with a particular poem or song, point out some of the words that start with the same sound. For example, after several readings of *Higglety Pigglety Pop!* (Sendak, 1979), you might point out that the words *pigglety*, *pop*, and *pig* all sound alike at the beginning and all start with the letter *p*. After noting the similarity between the way these words sound and look, you might say another word, such as *park*, and ask the children whether they think *park* begins like *pigglety*, *pop*, and *pig* and whether they think it would also begin with *p*. When everyone agrees that it does begin with *p*, then write the word on the board so the children can see it for themselves. Do this with one or two other such words.

Remember that your purpose is to help children link the beginning sounds of words they have learned orally to the visual representations of those sounds (i.e., phonemic awareness linked to print). In this kind of activity, it is not important that children learn any specific sound–symbol relationship. Instead, it is important that they begin to understand the alphabetic principle—that there is a relationship between the individual sounds in words and the letters that represent those sounds. You should vary the forms of text in which you look for these relationships.

How to Accommodate Differences

Accommodations for English Language Learners

Children who are English language learners often need additional support in order to get the most benefit from early literacy instruction (Ford, 2010; Tabors, 2008; Yesil-Dagli, 2011). Tabors (2008, p. 25) offers five strategies for use with English language learners in early childhood settings:

1. Use lots of nonverbal communication.
2. Keep the message simple.
3. Talk about the here and now.
4. Emphasize the important words in a sentence.
5. Combine gestures with talk.

Suggestions such as these are useful for working with any young child but are particularly important when the language of instruction at school is other than the language spoken at home.

Accommodations for Atypical Learners

All children benefit from opportunities to return to familiar books on their own. Many 3- and 4-year-olds actually memorize parts of books that have been read over and over to them. Providing little-book versions of the Big Books read at school can help this memorization take place. Little books can also be sent home for sharing with members of the family. For the child who is developing more slowly than most, books for promoting phonemic awareness should be read several times at school before they are sent home. Bringing home a familiar book builds a child's confidence because he or she can share the book with family members, listen and participate as the book is read aloud, and talk about the story.

Accommodations for Advanced Learners

Whenever possible, provide small copies of the Big Books you share with children. These "little books" are often packaged in sets of six. Encourage your advanced learners to "read" the books on their own. You will find that they will be the first to memorize whole texts and to ask about specific words, phrases, and letters.

FOCUSED STRATEGIES FOR SHARED READING

The focused strategies that follow are designed to call children's attention to specific aspects of print. They move children beyond print awareness to active exploration of the sounds of language, manipulation of print, and exploration of connections between letters and sounds.

Focused Strategy 1: Clapping Our Names

Children are usually keenly interested in their own names. This strategy is engaging for children as it requires them to clap the number of parts (syllables) they hear in their names (Yopp & Yopp, 2000).

What It Does

Clapping the number of parts in a name requires that children listen carefully to separate the syllables they hear. This is not something that children naturally listen for or do on their own. This activity introduces children to the important concept that some words have more than one part and that these parts (syllables) can be counted.

How to Do It

Step 1. Tell children that you have been thinking about their names and how they sound: "Some names, such as *John*, have only one part or syllable. When I think of *John*, I think of clapping one time." Then say the name *John* and clap once. Repeat. "Other names, such as *Ki-ki* (Kiki), have two parts. So when I think of *Ki-ki*, I clap two times." Say the name *Kiki* and clap two times. Repeat.

Step 2. After demonstrating with a few more names, invite the children to clap some names with you, as illustrated in Figure 4.2. Begin by using only one- and two-syllable names. When you think the children have caught on, advance to names with more than two syllables. Continue with this phonemic awareness activity as a brief part of large-group time. When most children are capable of listening to and clapping the parts of names, in particular their own, you might want to show a printed name after it has been clapped. The children will learn that they can say it, clap it, and read it.

Step 3. Engage children in making a class book. You will need a sheet of paper for each child, some small scraps of colored paper, and some paste or glue. Invite the children to each draw a self-portrait on a separate sheet of paper. Have the children sign their drawings. Then ask each child to say his or her name aloud, count

FIGURE 4.2. Clapping names.

the syllables, and select one paper scrap for each syllable. Have the children paste the paper scraps on their self-portrait pages. Compile the pages into a class book (see Figure 4.3). Read the book with the children during large-group time; then place it in the library center for children's independent exploration.

Variation

Clapping Other Words. To help children discover that they can clap the syllables for any word they know, select a word or two from a shared writing exercise. Have the children clap the syllables.

How to Accommodate Differences

Accommodations for English Language Learners. Clapping names or words may be done in any language. Try clapping syllables for names and words in the children's home languages other than English.

Accommodations for Atypical Learners. Most children can learn this activity fairly easily. Nevertheless, some children have considerable difficulty attending to any level of sounds in words. Clapping names is a good activity for informal screening of such difficulties. After several lessons, notice which children still seem to have difficulty. Find a quiet place and spend a brief time with them one-on-one. You may find that these children are confused by all the clapping or do not understand

FIGURE 4.3. "Clap Your Name" book.

the directions. They may have problems listening attentively or separating syllables. They may be confused because they are mispronouncing a word. Try to determine where the problem lies. Children may need to work one-on-one with a teacher several times before they fully understand the activity.

Accommodations for Advanced Learners. Advanced learners will begin to notice that some words are long and are likely to have more syllables. Try having them read a few pages of the class book with you. Cover the paper scraps pasted on each page. If necessary, help the children to read the name. Then ask the children to count and clap the number of parts in it. Finally, show them the pieces of paper pasted on the page to check their work. Keep in mind that it is not necessary for the children to be able to read the names. You can read the names and have the children listen for the number of syllables.

Focused Strategy 2: Matching Beginning Sounds

When children begin to develop the alphabetic principle, they typically attend first to initial sounds in words. This strategy takes advantage of and supports that inclination to attend to sounds in words.

What It Does

Children learn to listen to the sounds at the beginnings of words and to categorize words according to their beginning sounds. This activity is a precursor to the center-based activity that follows.

How to Do It

Step 1. Ask children to listen to several words that begin with the same sound (e.g., *Sam*, *sip*, and *sock*). Repeat the words, emphasizing the beginning sound. Point out that all of these words begin with the same sound, /s/. Then repeat the words once again.

Step 2. Tell the children that you are going to say another word and think about whether or not it begins like *Sam*, *sip*, and *sock*. Say, "The word I am thinking of is *sick*. Let me see. Does it start like *Sam*, *sip*, and *sock*? Yes, it does. Now I am going to try another word." Continue with other words, such as *sale*, *summer*, and *seal*. Each time go back and say the keywords, *Sam*, *sip*, and *sock*, and then the new word. After modeling two or three times, invite the children to participate. Try at least one word that does not begin with /s/.

Step 3. Play the game for a second or third time on subsequent days. Modeling for the children, say, "We know these words sound the same at the beginning. I wonder how they look at the beginning. I will write them down to take a look." Write the words *Sam*, *sip*, and *sock* on a chalkboard or chart paper, stressing the sound of the letter *s*. Have the children "read" the words with you. Guide them in noticing that the words all look the same at the beginning. The letter they begin with is the letter *s*. Point out that *Sam* begins with the uppercase *S* and *sip* and *sock* with the lowercase *s*, but they all begin with the same letter.

Step 4. It is important to teach only one letter and its corresponding sound at a time. Instruction should be very brief, simple, and easy for most children to grasp. Keep in mind that the objective of this activity extends beyond learning about the sound–symbol relationship of /s/. The larger goal is to have children understand something about how English works—that sounds in words can be written with letters. Once they realize that there are sound–symbol relationships, they can generalize this idea to match other letters with sounds.

Variations

Matching Beginning Sounds Using Pictures. When most children seem to understand how sounds and letters go together, try this variation. Cut pictures from magazines or draw simple pictures of familiar objects. Paste a picture of an object whose name begins with the target sound at the top of a piece of chart paper. Write the name of the object next to it. For example, draw a picture of a sock and write the word *sock* next to it. One at a time, show the pictures and have children decide whether or not the objects' names begin with the same sound as *sock*. If so, the objects can be pasted on the chart. Note that objects are often called by many names (e.g., *bucket* vs. *pail*; *carton* vs. *box*; *bag* vs. *sack*). You may need to guide children to name the word you have in mind.

Some sound–letter relationships appear to be easier to learn than others. For instance, children usually find it easy to link letter names and sounds when the name of the letter contains the sound (e.g., *b*, *m*, *p*, *s*, and *t*).

Make sure that the words you choose begin with single consonant sounds. Avoid words that begin with consonant blends and digraphs. The beginning sounds of these words cannot be linked to a single letter. Here are some sample word sets to get you started: *bake*, *bug*, and *boat*; *mop*, *milk*, and *make*; *top*, *toes*, and *tent*.

How to Accommodate Differences

Accommodations for English Language Learners. Assuming that English is the language of instruction, it is important that children pronounce the words in standard English if they are to make the correct sound–letter match. Speak clearly and distinctly as you introduce English words and sounds, and have the children repeat after you. Although this kind of lesson can be applied to any alphabetic language, sound–letter correspondence does vary among languages. For preschool children, stick to simple English sound–letter relationships so that children understand the principle involved.

Accommodations for Atypical Learners. Sound–letter correspondence is a challenging concept for many children. For some, the issue is time. Atypical learners need more time than most children to grasp concepts and apply them successfully. Individual and small-group activities will help keep them from falling far behind. Keep in mind that the lower your student-to-teacher ratio, the more likely you are to capture and keep children's attention.

Accommodations for Advanced Learners. Many children who are advanced learners seem to figure out sound–letter correspondence independently. They tend to see patterns more easily than other children. They discover, either on their own or by having someone point it out, that some words share the same beginning sound and that these words also share the same beginning letters. For instance, Billy figures out that *ball* and *basket* have the same beginning sound as his name, and he learns that all three words begin with the letter *b*. He gradually discovers a similar pattern with other sounds and letters. After many formal experiences with print, children like Billy begin to experiment with what they know. These early experiments often take the form of invented spelling. Chapter 5 will provide detailed explanation of children's use of alphabetic knowledge for spelling and writing.

Figure 4.4 is a self-portrait by a child who is demonstrating awareness of beginning letter sounds. She labeled it with the letters *B* and *D* and read, "My bike and doll" and then explained that the picture shows her playing with her bike and

FIGURE 4.4. Self-portrait with initial letter sounds.

doll. Children with this level of skill benefit from encouragement (but not pressure) to use what they know in their attempts at reading and writing.

Focused Strategy 3: Sorting Picture Cards

Children apply their knowledge of beginning sounds to sort pictures. This strategy should follow an abundance of whole-class and small-group activities of the type described in the previous strategy. By observing children in group activities, you will be able to determine when individual children are ready to move into independent work in learning centers.

What It Does

This strategy strengthens children's ability to distinguish the initial sounds in words and reinforces their understanding of the connection between sounds and letters.

How to Do It

Step 1. Before helping children sort pictures according to initial sound, you need to help them understand what sorting is all about. You will need pictures of items in several categories such as clothes, toys, and animals. These pictures can be drawn or found in books dealing with word study (e.g., Bear, Invernizzi, Templeton, & Johnston, 2000). When introducing picture-card sorting, it helps to designate one picture as a key picture that represents the category. For instance, if children are to sort pictures of clothing, you might draw a dress on red paper and draw the remaining clothing items on white paper. Children can then group the pictures of clothing with the dress. You will also need additional pictures that represent the beginning sounds that you have studied. For example, for the letter *b*, you might use a key picture of a ball. Other pictures might include a bat, a bone, a boy, and a bee.

Step 2. Introduce this activity by modeling the concept of sorting, using categories familiar to the children. For example, you might select clothing and toys. Attach a picture representing each category to the top of a two-column chart, using double-sided tape. Scramble the remaining items on a tabletop. Point out the two pictures on the chart and ask the children to tell you which is a toy and which is a piece of clothing. Explain that there are several pictures in the pile on the table and you are going to sort them according to whether they are clothes, toys, or something else. Hold up the first item and think aloud, "This is a doll. It is a toy, so I will stick it under the toy on the chart." Invite the children to help you sort the remaining pictures. Depending on the group, you might want to practice concept sorting with other common categories (such as food, things used for travel, or animals) before you introduce sorting by sounds.

Step 3. When most of the children have a good understanding of how a sorting game is played, model sorting familiar picture cards according to initial sound. Remind the children that they have been sorting lots of things they know, both as a group and independently in learning centers. This time, instead of paying attention to what category the picture belongs to, they will need to pay attention to the first sound in the name of the object.

Step 4. Demonstrate the process using a sound you have already discussed. Place the pictures for sorting in a plastic bag or an envelope. Dump them on a table and spread them out so that they can be seen easily. At first, it is a good idea to have all but one of the picture cards begin with the focus sound. For example, for the letter *p*, you might use a picture of a pig for the key card and pictures of a pin, a pail, a pipe, a pie, and a man for sorting. Children will then identify the pictures that have the same beginning sound as *pig* and find the one that does not fit.

Step 5. Be sure to model the process of naming each object with the children so they are calling it by the correct name. Say aloud the name of the object on the key picture card with each word for sorting before a decision is made. You might want to isolate the first sound before saying the word, for example, "/p/, *pig*; /p/, *pin*. Yes, they both sound the same at the very beginning. *Pig, pail.* Yes, they both sound the same at the beginning." After several weeks of modeling this activity with the group, place the materials in a learning center for children to sort on their own.

Step 6. To help the children connect sounds with letters, label the key card. Encourage children to notice that all the pictures sound the same at the beginning and start with the same letter as the key word. Then name the letter. Figure 4.5 shows a child's completed picture sort for beginning sounds. Note that a card featuring a question mark may be used to indicate where a child might put the card or cards that do not fit.

Step 7. Note that when teaching sorting, it is important to work with the whole group for short periods of time over many months before moving to a center-based activity. Notice which children are ready to sort independently and invite children to sort in a learning center when they are ready. Choose familiar sounds and sort for only one sound at a time. When a child sorts incorrectly, ask, "Why did you put this picture here?" Have the child name the picture. Gradually add more of the sounds you have introduced; when children are ready, add more than one word that does not fit the category.

FIGURE 4.5. Preschool child's completed sorting activity.

Variation

Picture Card Game. Create a card game designed for two or three children to play in which a pile of cards with pictures on them much like the ones in Figure 4.5 are placed face down on the table or desk. Children take turns taking cards from the deck. If the card has a picture that begins like the target sound, they may keep it. Otherwise it goes in a discard box or basket. When all the cards have been taken, the child with the most cards is the winner. Children can help check one another. Also, the teacher might take a quick look at the end of the game to see that the children have made correct decisions.

How to Accommodate Differences

Accommodations for English Language Learners. Pay special attention to any vocabulary and pronunciation differences that might interfere with the ability of English language learners to name the pictures and sort them into the correct category. Try to anticipate which children might have problems, and give them help in advance.

Accommodations for Atypical Learners. Some children need more practice in sorting by concept than others. Categorization is a high-level cognitive operation that is used throughout the preschool curriculum. Make certain that children understand what it means to sort things into similar categories so that they are not struggling with this basic concept at the same time they are attempting to sort the beginning sounds of words. For some children, the difficulty may result from limited background knowledge of the names of the pictures to be sorted. For others, the differences between sounds may be subtle or indistinguishable at first. Try to determine what the problem might be and then ease these children into sorting by sounds through one-on-one intervention.

Accommodations for Advanced Learners. Children who are advanced learners may enjoy the challenge of sorting two sounds. You might set out two key picture cards, each representing a different initial sound. Provide cards that fit into these categories, along with some that do not. The sorting chart shown in Figure 4.6 features three columns of cards, one for each sound and one with a question mark for those picture cards that do not fit.

NAME GAMES: AN INTEGRATED INSTRUCTIONAL STRATEGY

The focused strategies described thus far for use with shared reading included some that made use of children's names to help them understand specific print and alphabetic concepts, including syllables and beginning sounds. Here, we describe use of children's names as an integrated strategy to address concepts specifically

FIGURE 4.6. Advanced sorting chart.

focused on alphabet knowledge. Like shared reading, this strategy addresses alphabet knowledge within a broader framework of literacy activities, including direct systematic instruction of letter names and sounds. It serves as a model for the kind of activities that teachers should use throughout the year.

What the Name Game Does

Using children's names to teach them about print is a sure way to get their attention and keep their interest. Most children learn the letters of their name before they learn any others. Children's natural desire to read, spell, and write their names offers teachers a perfect opportunity to help children explore almost all the concepts of print.

Name games are activities that progress from easy to more difficult. Like shared reading, this strategy is meant to be used over an extended period of time. Teachers can assess children's progress and either repeat activities or stretch children to new challenges. Name games require only a few minutes at a time and are easily integrated into large-group time devoted to shared reading and other literacy activities.

How to Do Name Games

Begin by making a pair of identical name cards for each child in the class. Add helping pictures—photos of the children, stickers, or drawings—to the cards if you wish.

Name Match

Sort the cards into two sets. During large-group time, give each child a name card with his or her name on it. Hold up one card at a time from your set and ask, "Whose name is this?" Have the children match their cards with the card you are holding.

At first, the children will use the helping pictures to match. This is fine. The purpose of this game is to help them visually match items and learn the format of this large-group matching game, which will be the basis for other name games. After children get the idea of how the game is played, remove the part of the name card with the helping picture. Then have children match cards using only the print. Each time a child matches cards, recite the letters in his or her name. Invite the child to say the letters along with you as you point to them.

Who's Here?

Hang a strip of Velcro at children's eye level in a convenient spot in the classroom. Attach matching Velcro strips to the backs of one set of name cards. Place the name cards in a large shallow box or on a shelf near the hanging Velcro strip.

When children come in each morning, ask them to find their name cards and attach them to the hanging Velcro strip. During circle time, read the names together, as in Figure 4.7, to see who is present and who is absent. Select one or two names to read a second time, pointing to each letter as you go and encouraging children to join in. Now and then, repeat this activity in small groups or with individuals.

FIGURE 4.7. "Who's Here" name game.

Guess the Name

Once children are somewhat familiar with their names, hold up a name card, and cover all but the first letter. Ask questions such as "Whose name could this be? It starts with the letter *J*. Charles, could this be your name? Jason, could this be your name? Who else's name could this be? Joshua? Carla?" Reveal more letters and continue in the same way. At first, do this while children are holding their copies of the name cards. Encourage them to compare the letters on their name cards to those on the card you are holding. When most of the children seem to understand the process and can identify their names, try holding on to their copies of the name cards to see if they can identify their names from memory. Ask questions about the names of the letters you are revealing.

Name Puzzle

Print each child's name on a business-size envelope. Make a duplicate on a piece of oaktag or stiff paper. Cut the duplicate into individual letters and place them inside the envelope. Have each child match the cut letters to the name on the outside of the envelope. Be sure to model this process during large-group time before you ask children to do this on their own. Again, name the letters when you are modeling for the children. After children have reconstructed their names with the cut-apart letters in the envelopes, assist them in spelling their names aloud (see Figure 4.8).

FIGURE 4.8. Reconstructing names.

Letter Detectives

Display one, two, or three name cards at a time. It is best to start with one name card and work up to three once children have the idea. Show a letter card and identify the letter. Ask "Can you find this letter in any of these names?" Many children will be able to visually match letters that are not in their names, although they may not be able to identify those letters in isolation. This is a good beginning.

For an additional challenge, ask children to find two names that have the same first letter, find two names that have the same last letter, or find the name that contains a particular letter. (This would be done without showing the letter.) Note that children need to understand the positional words *first* and *last* in order to do this activity. To assist children with this important concept, point to the beginning of the word as you say *first* and to the end of the word when you say *last*.

In the name games collection of activities, teachers model essential literacy behaviors, encourage children's involvement, and support the development of print concepts. The games progress from easy to difficult; each is scaffolded so that the teacher models, invites children to participate, and then encourages them to work independently as he or she monitors their progress. Here is a list of name game tasks in order of increasing difficulty:

- Recognize name with graphic support (photo or sticker).
- Recognize name without graphic support.
- Apply name recognition purposefully.
- Differentiate between and among names.
- Reconstruct own name from individual letters.
- Visually match specific letters in names.
- From a set of three names, find the two names that begin or end with the same letter.
- Look at a letter and find the name that has the letter at the beginning, end, or somewhere in the middle.

Variations

Writing Children's Names

Find opportunities to write children's names each day. Be sure to spell aloud as you write and invite children to spell with you. Even when children write their own names, it is important to name the letters with them.

Hunting for Letters

Have children find the letters in their names, particularly the first letter, in other places in the room, such as in alphabet books, on charts, and so on.

Letter Games

Once children have demonstrated sufficient understanding of name game activities, try some of the following variations:

- Show a letter and have children name it.
- Name a letter without showing it and have children find a name with that letter.
- Ask one child to name a letter and another child to find it.
- Say a word not on the list, stressing its initial sound. Have children locate a name on the list that has the same beginning sound.

Finding Names on a Helpers Chart

Name games can be adapted for use with a helpers chart in which children's name cards are used to indicate classroom chore assignments. Notice which children recognize their own names and those of their classmates.

How to Accommodate Differences

Accommodations for English Language Learners

Name games work with names from any language because all children identify with their names. Avoid Anglicizing a child's name (e.g., referring to "Enrique"—pronounced *en re kay*—as "Henry") to make it easier for you to pronounce.

Accommodations for Atypical Learners

Children who are developing more slowly than most might benefit from more tactile experiences. Forming their names with plastic letters or other types of three-dimensional letters can help them develop alphabet knowledge.

Accommodations for Advanced Learners

Children who know most of the letters of the alphabet should be encouraged to develop accuracy and fluency through bingo, lotto, and other games that make use of the alphabet. They may also sing songs such as "B-I-N-G-O" and change the first letter to Z or W to extend their alphabet knowledge. They should also be encouraged to write just for fun. However, keep in mind that some children's intellectual abilities may be far ahead of their fine-motor skills.

FOCUSED STRATEGIES FOR NAME GAMES

As with the focused strategies used in conjunction with shared reading, more focused strategies can also be used to help children attend to print beyond that found in their own names. The focused strategies that follow will help children develop alphabetic knowledge.

Focused Strategy 1: Sharing Alphabet Books

What It Does

Regular exposure to alphabet books during read-aloud time is essential to supporting children's learning of letter names. Alphabet books can also be used to support their developing knowledge of letter–sound correspondence.

How to Do It

Step 1. Over time, try to add a variety of types of alphabet books to your library collection. Obtain at least two copies of each alphabet book. Use one copy for read-alouds and make the other copies accessible to the children. Alphabet books in enlarged text format (i.e., Big Books) with companion sets of little books are particularly useful. *Chicka Chicka Boom Boom* (Archambault & Martin, 2000) and *On Market Street* (Lobel, 1981) are two excellent alphabet books available in Big Book format.

Step 2. Throughout the year, introduce a new alphabet book every few weeks or so. Keep in mind that alphabet books can also be selected to complement topics of study, as was illustrated in Chapter 3 by a teachers' use of a construction alphabet book. Between new books, continue to return periodically to books already read.

Step 3. When using Big Books with companion sets of little books, allow two or three of the little books to be taken home for read-alouds with parents. The books can be placed in a plastic bag and be part of a take-home book circulation program.

Step 4. Use the alphabet books in conjunction with the following activities:

- Have children indicate letters from the books that they know in their own names and in the names of others.
- Have children match letters from alphabet books with letters on a large wall alphabet chart placed at the children's eye level.
- Compare alphabet books in terms of the illustrations and special features (e.g., rhyme, themes). Have children tell which ones they like best and why.

Variations

Reading with a Partner. Divide the children into pairs. Distribute a copy of a familiar alphabet book to each pair, or allow pairs to select a book of their choice. Tell them that today they are going to have fun reading together. They can take turns looking through the book page by page, or they can each hunt for letters they know and read the pages on which those letters appear. First, they should read the letter, and then they can tell about anything else they see on the page. Model the process for them, and then have two children demonstrate. Have each pair find a comfortable spot in the room to read. Use the opportunity to circulate among the children and observe evidence of their understandings about print (e.g., naming letters or handling books). This activity offers children an opportunity to engage in literacy in a social way. It is especially helpful for children who rarely visit the library center on their own but enjoy working with others. Children can also try this activity alone or in groups of three.

How to Accommodate Differences

Accommodations for English Language Learners. Ask a librarian about alphabet books in other languages. You may not feel comfortable reading them, and they may not be appropriate for your entire class; however, you might want to make parents and other caregivers aware of the books' availability. Keep in mind that what children learn about concepts of print in one language can be applied to a second language.

Accommodations for Atypical Learners. All children enjoy hearing the same book over and over again. For children who are developing more slowly than most, repeated readings of the same alphabet book can be very beneficial. Encourage parents and other home caregivers to read a particular alphabet book to their children each night. Parents who have limited literacy skills often feel comfortable with this type of activity. Encourage them to let their children take the lead as often as possible.

Accommodations for Advanced Learners. As mentioned earlier, it is important to offer children a range of alphabet books. Advanced learners will enjoy reading and browsing through the more complex alphabet books in your collection.

Focused Strategy 2: Making a Class Alphabet Book

This strategy engages children in creating a class alphabet book. It encourages children to notice the structure and conventions of alphabet books while also focusing their attention on individual alphabet letters.

What It Does

Creation of an alphabet book helps children apply what they have learned through exposure to professionally written alphabet books. In addition to reinforcing their alphabet knowledge, children make use of virtually all they know about books and concepts of print.

How to Do It

Step 1. Briefly show one or two of the alphabet books with which the children are familiar. Call attention to how the books are similar and how they are different. Invite the children to make their own class alphabet book.

Step 2. Explain that the children will need to make some decisions: How many letters will appear on each page of their book? Will the letters appear in a particular order? How will the children verify that order? By checking various sources (alphabet books and charts), the children can see that there is a certain order to the alphabet.

Step 3. Allow one page per alphabet letter. Print the letter in both uppercase and lowercase at the top of the page. Have the children illustrate each page with drawings or magazine pictures of things whose names begin with that letter. Decide whether you want to label the pictures. If so, print clearly and spell out the words as you write them.

Step 4. This project should continue over several months. Use sturdy paper and rings to hold the pages together. Make the book accessible to the children.

Step 5. During large-group time, periodically reread to the children the pages that have been completed. Then return the book to the library center for children to read on their own.

Variation

Personal Alphabet Books. After completing the class alphabet book, encourage children to create their own alphabet books. Children may choose to illustrate the pages of their books or paste a cut-out magazine picture on each page. Have the children label the pages using whatever forms of writing they wish. As will be explained in Chapter 5, preschool children typically use a variety of forms including scribbles, a mix of invented and conventional alphabet letters, or entirely conventional letters. Often children will use whatever letters they know to represent what they want to say. For most children, this is the first step in the process toward achieving more conventional writing.

Individual alphabet books can be done in conjunction with the class book. Each time new letters are introduced to the class, children can follow up with pages in their personal books. If an iPad or other tablet technology is available for children's use, consider allowing them to create electronic versions of their individual alphabet books. Some children will find it easier to write with a fingertip than with a pencil or marker. Others simply may be more attracted to digital creation of alphabet book pages.

How to Accommodate Differences

Accommodations for English Language Learners. Occasionally label an illustration with a word from another language that shares most letters of the English alphabet as well as with the English word. Show how the same letters can be used to write in both languages.

Accommodations for Atypical Learners. For children who are developing more slowly than most, recognizing letters and remembering letter names will take much more time. Concentrate on the letters in each child's name first. Gradually extend to other words important to the child: *mom*, *dad*, names of siblings, and so on.

Accommodations for Advanced Learners. Many children will know all of the upper- and lowercase letters by the age of 4. Focus children's attention on the first letter of the labeled words and to the sounds the letters represent, when applicable.

Focused Strategy 3: Using Digital Technology to Enhance Alphabet Knowledge

This strategy requires children to use computers or other digital technologies to extend and reinforce their alphabet knowledge.

What It Does

Technology-based activities offer children an opportunity to practice skills in engaging and varied ways. Alphabet activities to suit the level of virtually all preschool children are widely available on the Internet or as free apps for smartphones and tablets. Some current websites that offer alphabet activities include the following:

- Public Broadcasting System: *www.pbs.org*
- Reading Is Fundamental: *www.rif.org*
- Sesame Street: *www.sesameworkshop.org*
- U.S. Department of Education: *www.ed.gov*

Blogs on these websites and some of the websites themselves frequently include reviews of early literacy apps. These range from games that entail sorting and matching letters to interactive digital storybooks with features that highlight and allow manipulation of print as children are reading.

Always preview computer program and apps in advance and plan for their use. Consider how you will introduce the activity, the length of time you want a child to work at a particular activity, whether the activity is more effective if children work individually or in pairs, and how you might vary its use according to student needs and abilities.

Introduce new software or apps to the entire group, perhaps demonstrating on a digital whiteboard if one is available, letting some children participate in the demonstration as you guide them. Move gradually to independent center-based work by first selecting children who can work alone with very little guidance. This will give others an opportunity to get a feel for what is involved in the activity. As other children are selected, give them a brief tutorial as they begin.

Variations

Take advantage of the variations built into the computer software and apps. Adjust the software settings to match the children's abilities. Young children will need guidance in finding the level most appropriate for them. Note that in order to take advantage of software variations, it is important that you review the software carefully before introducing it to the group.

Ask yourself the following questions as you observe children engaged in digital technology activities:

- Is there evidence that the child is gaining a sense of control over the medium of instruction (i.e., the computer or tablet)?
- Is the child following instructions and giving mostly appropriate responses?
- Does the child self-correct when the wrong response is made?
- Does the child seem to be gaining confidence about his or her alphabet knowledge?
- Is there some evidence of connection between what the child is learning via the technology and what he or she is learning in other classroom activities?

How to Accommodate Differences

Accommodations for English Language Learners. Most computer activities and apps to which American teachers have access are in English. Children tend to adapt easily to these materials, but English language learners might benefit from extra help to get them started. If someone is available who speaks the children's home language, arrange for that person to give English language learners a brief tutorial.

One advantage of digital technology is the inclusion of recorded voices that read aloud e-books written in other languages. Seeking out books in children's native languages can provide them with models of their own language read aloud while corresponding text is highlighted, a feature that is especially useful when teachers do not know the languages of all of the children in their classrooms.

Accommodations for Atypical Learners. Offer a range of digital materials to accommodate children who are developing more slowly than most. It is very important that all children gain a sense of success and accomplishment from the activities in which they engage. Seek out programs and apps with multiple levels of difficulty so that all children can find success at a level that matches their skill.

Accommodations for Advanced Learners. As with all children, the advanced learner needs to be challenged but not frustrated. These children are most likely to want new materials to explore. They should be encouraged to use levels of materials that require great levels of skills development. Some may also be able to use the computer in more conventional ways, including composing using the keyboard or typing into e-books they create themselves using text-typing functions instead of writing with their fingers on a touch screen.

MAKING CONNECTIONS BETWEEN HOME AND SCHOOL

In Chapter 2 we discussed the home as an important context for early literacy development and learning. While encouraging parents to enhance the literacy environment at home by making reading and writing materials available and by engaging children in parents' everyday functional uses of print, teachers can also suggest activities that will help children develop alphabetic knowledge.

Use the information in Figures 4.9 and 4.10 to create your own fliers to be sent home to parents or for use at a parents meeting. Prepare the fliers in more than one language if necessary.

In school we are learning about letters. We are discovering that . . .

- The letters of the alphabet are used to make words.
- We can learn the names of all the letters.
- We can learn the letters in our name.

Learning about letters is important because . . .

- Knowing the alphabet gives children an advantage in learning to read and write.
- Letter names are part of the language used to talk about reading and writing.
- Knowledge of letters is helpful in learning how letters and sounds relate to one another (phonics) and helps children to remember how words are spelled.

Here are a few ways you can help:

- Sing the alphabet song with your child.
- Read alphabet books to your child and point to the letters on each page as you name them.
- Display your child's name in a prominent place and help him or her learn the letters.
- Provide alphabet blocks or magnetic letters for your child to play with.

FIGURE 4.9. Information for parents: Learning about letters.

From *Reading and Writing in Preschool: Teaching the Essentials* by Renée M. Casbergue and Dorothy S. Strickland. Copyright 2016 by The Guilford Press. Permission to photocopy this figure is granted to purchasers of this book for personal use only (see copyright page for details). Purchasers can download a larger version of this figure (see the box at the end of the table of contents).

Myths about Phonemic Awareness, Concepts of Print, and Alphabet Knowledge

Once children have developed phonemic awareness and can isolate sounds in spoken language, they will naturally use that awareness to make sense of print.

Phonemic awareness represents a critically important step in children's language and literacy development. It is a specialized preliteracy skill that comes quite naturally to some, but not most, children. Even for those who develop phonemic awareness quite easily, however, the connections between sounds and print must be demonstrated. Preschool children typically do not have highly developed metacognitive ability—they often are not consciously aware of what they know about the language they use every day. Until children become consciously aware of individual sounds in language and learn to manipulate those sounds, they cannot apply that knowledge to engagement with print with any intentionality. Thus, all children need assistance both to develop conscious phonemic awareness and to see the connections between language sounds and the print that represents it.

We are learning about books and print. Your child is learning the following concepts:
- The print around us has meaning.
- When we think and talk about the things we do, what we say can be written down and read back to us. The print tells the reader what to say.
- Reading and writing let people do many things such as enjoy a story, read a menu, or write a note.

Learning about books and print is important for many reasons:
- The more children know about how print works, the more they will be eager and ready to learn to read.
- They will possess knowledge of basic concepts required for reading and writing.

Here are some ways that you can help:
- Read to your child and encourage him or her to browse independently through books that you have read aloud.
- Show the ways that you use reading and writing in your daily life: writing notes and grocery lists; reading books, magazines, and newspapers; or finding information online.

FIGURE 4.10. Information for parents: Learning about books and print.

From *Reading and Writing in Preschool: Teaching the Essentials* by Renée M. Casbergue and Dorothy S. Strickland. Copyright 2016 by The Guilford Press. Permission to photocopy this figure is granted to purchasers of this book for personal use only (see copyright page for details). Purchasers can download a larger version of this figure (see the box at the end of the table of contents)

It is best to introduce one letter each week to children. This lets them focus on the features of that single letter and consolidate their knowledge of the letter and its sound for a full week before another letter is introduced.

While curricula that introduce one letter per week have been commonplace, more recently the "letter of the week" approach has come under considerable criticism. Children certainly require concentrated attention to individual letters and sufficient time to master letter names and sounds. Introducing one letter per week, however, means that it will take children a full 26 weeks to be introduced to all of the letters. Most children are capable of learning the alphabet more rapidly with appropriate instruction. Moreover, learning one letter at a time does not require children to discriminate one letter from another. If a whole week is spent learning about "Mr. M" and children are prompted to respond with the letter name M and the sound /m/ each time they are prompted with the letter or pictures of words that begin with that letter, most children will very quickly learn to parrot back the correct response. This is not, however, an indication that they have actually mastered recognition of that letter or knowledge of its corresponding sound. Introducing two or three contrasting letters at a time and pointing out how they are alike and different is likely to lead to deeper learning. McGee (2007) has suggested groupings of three letters to teach together based on their physical features, groupings that she found to be effective over many years in multiple preschool classrooms involved in different Early Reading First projects.

IDEAS FOR DISCUSSION, REFLECTION, AND ACTION

1. Discuss the strategies offered in this chapter. In what ways are they similar to or different from things you are already doing? Discuss any changes you might make to your curriculum.

2. Observe a demonstration of a lesson that focuses on phonemic awareness. The demonstration may be provided by a fellow teacher or someone leading the professional development effort in your school. It may be done with children, simulated without children, or it may make use of a video that fits with the ideas and strategies offered in the chapter. Keep the chapter content in mind as you participate in a discussion of examples from the demonstration that illustrate understanding about language and literacy development, effective teaching, and connections to your district- or school-based standards and assessment.

3. Begin collecting alphabet books that can be used to teach alphabet knowledge and support children's learning of the alphabetic principle. Be sure to seek out alphabet books that fit themes of study in your curriculum or that enhance children's investigation of concepts in science and social studies.

4. Examine any Big Books available for use in your classroom. Note the structure of the book and the language used. Determine which print-related concepts can be most easily taught using each book. Then plan interactive shared reading activities to help children develop those concepts using the books as anchors for the lessons.

CHAPTER 5

Developing Alphabetic Knowledge for Writing

Toward the end of the year in preschool, 5-year-old Bella worked on an iPad in the writing center to create a page for an e-book about her family. She tapped the "+" sign at the top of the screen and easily selected "add photo" with its photo icon from the drop-down menu. She then selected a picture of her little brother from the photo folder that popped up, and tapped the photo to insert it onto the blank page. Using her finger on the screen, she wrote three letters beneath the photograph: *M B B*. She pointed to individual letters as she read, "My [pointing to the *M*], ba- [pointing to the first *B*], be [pointing to the second *B*]." She hastily added another *B*, saying, "brother." She then reread, again pointing to each letter, "My ba-by brother."

Bella's process as she created this page for her e-book illustrates that she is well on her way to understanding how print functions to convey meaning. She began with a clear purpose, selected a relevant photograph, and utilized a corresponding form—a caption for the picture—to convey what she wanted to say. She used actual alphabet letters exclusively, and selected letters by listening to beginning sounds in the words.

Her attempt to read what she had written is especially revealing about her use of the alphabetic principle. As we have described in earlier chapters, children demonstrate alphabetic knowledge when they make the connection between letters and sounds as they read and write. While Bella's writing was not conventional, we can see that she had reached a point in her writing development that enabled her to listen for sounds in the words she wants to use and represent those sounds with corresponding letters. Bella also demonstrated beginning understanding of the concept of word, representing each unit she perceived to be a word with a single letter. Her perception that "baby" is actually two separate words is typical of preschoolers who often can't distinguish whether parts of words they hear are separate words or syllables—at least until they have more experience seeing those words in print.

In Chapter 4, we described strategies to support children's development of alphabetic knowledge for reading. This chapter describes how children move toward using knowledge of alphabet letters and the alphabetic principle to grow as writers. We describe two concurrent journeys children take on their journey to becoming conventional writers—from scribbles to use of alphabet letters, and from nonphonemic choice of letters to alphabetic spelling—as they attempt to write words. This chapter will also detail the integrated strategy of shared writing to support writing development, and focused strategies that call children's attention to specific aspects of print.

THE JOURNEY FROM SCRIBBLES TO SCRIPT

The development of marks used for writing begins with children's first intentional use of lines intended as writing. The development we consider here typically spans from 2 or 2½ years of age to a little over 5 years of age—from the late toddler stage through the end of the preschool years (Baghban, 1984; Clay, 1987; Schickedanz, 1990).

The First Discovery: "I Can Make Marks"

Writing materials and the physical forms of writing and drawing fascinate young children. Children's discovery that writing and drawing tools leave tracks and that the form of the tracks is under their control sparks curiosity. Anyone who has watched young children experiment with markers on a blank surface has observed how much fun they seem to have just experimenting with straight lines, arcs, and dots.

For several months, toddlers continue this type of exploration and take great delight in their actions no matter the results on the paper. Then, a question seems to occur to the exploring child: "How do I get that design again?" This question sometimes emerges as marks produced in free exploration begin to remind the child of something. Consider the drawing in Figure 5.1, which was created by a 2-year-old as he explored with a marker on white notepaper. The child was silent, absorbed in the doing, until he finished drawing. He looked a long time at this drawing, touched it several times, and then said, "A man." Then, he pointed to the

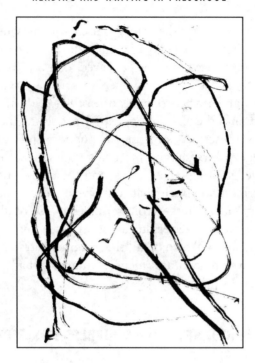

FIGURE 5.1. Beginning representational drawing.

two spots in the top portion and said, "Eyes," and next to the large inside circle in the middle and said, "Mouth."

It is doubtful that the child intended to create any specific design when he first put pen to paper. But suddenly, there it was—a happy accident—the result of a series of random, exploratory movements. With new interest in the marks, the child began to wonder, "I want to do that again, but how? What did I do to produce this?"

Marking becomes more deliberate after this question comes to the child's mind. Of course, not every occasion of marking is guided by such thoughts. Before 2½ or 3 years of age, the thought is probably rarely there as the child creates marks. The sheer joy of doing dominates the child's marking, and it remains a motivation for writing throughout the early childhood years. The difference, though, after some point in the third year of life, are the moments, and soon an ever-increasing number of them, when action is deliberate. The child wants to make a line look a certain way, or wants to create a particular form to represent a specific image. Or the child wants to make it clear that marks made on a specific occasion are not a picture of something, but "say" something. Marking and meaning become joined on these occasions of deliberate action to serve specific representational purposes. Sometimes, the representation is a picture; sometimes the marks are intended as writing.

This Is Writing, Not a Picture

If someone were to show you the two samples in Figure 5.2, odds are you would know at a glance that Figure 5.2a is writing. Figure 5.2b, on the other hand, might require some study: Did the form result from a child's random exploration with a marker, or was it intended to be a picture of something, such as a face with bangs covering the forehead, or a bowl of spaghetti with a noodle hanging over its edge? As it turns out, Figure 5.2b is a phone message, written by a 3-year-old in the midst of dramatic play.

The latter representation (Figure 5.2b) is typical of children who are at the very beginning of their journey into learning how to mark meanings. Early on, we see no difference between the marks the child uses to draw pictures and those that are intended to "say" something. We know the child's intention only by listening to what the child says or by watching the context in which the child applies the marking tool to paper or uses the item after its creation.

Almost on the heels of the dawning of representational intentions, however, we see evidence that the child now understands that marks used for writing look different from those used for drawing pictures. Figure 5.3 illustrates this insight. First, the child drew a scribble picture covering most of the paper's surface, using lines that went here and there and round and round. Then, the child placed marks

FIGURE 5.2. Two different ways of writing.

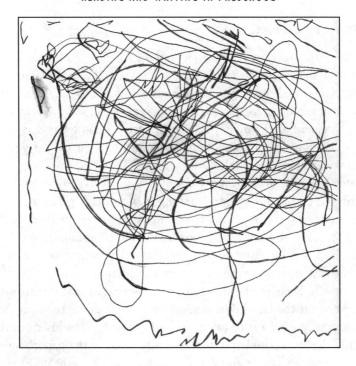

FIGURE 5.3. Drawing and early writing mixed.

at the bottom of the page and said they were her name (see the zigzag scribble writing there). These marks were separated a bit from the picture and arranged in a linear pattern. We also see some writing marks along the far left of the paper. These resemble the letters *J*, *l*, and *i*, all of which were used in the child's name. Though arranged vertically, not horizontally, on the page, as is the convention for English writing, the letters are in a line and stand apart from the scribbled picture.

The child exerted a different kind of control over the marks intended as writing than she applied to the lines in her drawing. Writing marks were not allowed to go all over the place. The internal variations in lines of the child's writing are fairly uniform, as if she had noticed that the same details repeat frequently in a way that details do not typically repeat in a picture since pictures contain greater variation in form than writing does. Clearly, the child who created this sample was aware of two general worlds of marks: a world of pictures and a world of print. This distinction is a major discovery for the young child.

Details, Details: Increasing Focus on the Features of Print Symbols

In the world of writing, individual designs—alphabet letters—make up the lines of print that children notice. At first, the line itself, the fact of a linear arrangement, is all that seems to register with young children. It is usually the only feature they try to capture in their writing. This, after all, is what makes a collection of marks *look* like writing and not a picture. For a while they represent this perception only with zigs and zags varying in density. The scribble lines making up the "letter to Daddy" shown in Figure 5.4a, for example, have very little variation. In contrast, the lines in Figure 5.4b, which were created by a 4-year-old who was playing at producing writing, have very dense zigs and zags that vary considerably. Even so, the child is still using *only* zigs and zags.

When we compare this writing with both Figures 5.4c and 5.4d, we notice something new in the last two. The marks in their lines of print contain not only a few zigs and zags but also some loops. In Figure 5.4c, the first line even starts with

FIGURE 5.4. Variations in linear writing.

a separate small form, a closed curve—a circle. There are a few other marks that stand alone: the small closed curve with a tail at the beginning of line five, and the small vertical line at the beginning of line six. In line four, we also can see that the child started with a zigzag that looks very much like W. It was followed with a closed curve (similar to O), not with another zigzag. This closed curve is followed by a zigzag line that is open at the bottom rather than at the top, which looks like M. The variation in the forms included here shows the child's awareness that lines of print are comprised of different symbols, an important step toward eventually noticing that lines of print are comprised of individual letters of the alphabet.

Figure 5.4d was created by the same 4-year-old who created Figure 5.4c. She turned over her paper to write "a letter." But here, she used almost no scribble writing. Many of these marks are mock letters, made up forms that have features of alphabet letters. The letters a, c, and e appeared in her name, Tracey, which adults in her family wrote in lowercase (as none of these letters was the first letter in her name). The noncurved lines in her name were t and y. We can see the influence of all these letters in the child's writing, although she also took some liberties. When writing her letters, she created some new forms that are not found in the English alphabet.

Mock letters contain the segments that are the building blocks of actual letters. To understand what children are probably thinking when they create mock letters, consider Legos, the popular construction toy. These toys are packaged with an insert that shows how to build a few specific constructions with the materials provided. Of course, the possibilities are vast and children invent many original designs, not just those shown in the package instructions. But no matter what a child builds, the basic materials of a construction toy make all the varied structures look like they belong together. They are of the same kind because the basic pieces used to make any item come from the same basic set of materials as are used to make other items.

A limited set of lines—building blocks—is also available to make all letters of the alphabet. Some lines are used in some letters; other lines are used in others. Often the same kinds of lines are used in many letters, but their number (compare E and F) or placement (compare d and b) vary. Creating letters is the same as creating structures with blocks—the possibilities for creating different forms are almost endless. The child does not know at first that there are only 26 letters—that all the possibilities for creating forms with this set of lines are not exploited. For all the child knows, there could be 50 or 100 letters in the English alphabet, just as there are endless possibilities for different block constructions from the same set of basic blocks. Until a child has several years of experience, including exposure to a variety of alphabet puzzles, alphabet books, and words in the environment, we are likely to see mock letters in the child's writing.

When a child builds with construction toys, teachers praise creativity and encourage unique constructions. With writing, the rules change—socialization narrows the possibilities. Eventually, the almost infinite number of possible marks is winnowed down to a standard set. During the preschool years, as children devise new letter forms, teachers must accept and celebrate their good thinking. In time, and rather quickly actually, children narrow the designs of their creations so that even mock letters look very much like actual letters.

Eventually, children come to realize that there is only a finite set of alphabet letters. This was the case for Mario one day, when, after finishing an alphabet puzzle, he asked his teacher, "Are these all the alphabet letters in the whole wide world?" She asked what made him think that this might be all of them. "Because," he said, "I see the same ones everywhere!" The teacher explained that the puzzle the child had just completed did indeed contain all the English alphabet letters in the whole wide world, but that there are other languages in the world with differ-ent alphabet symbols. This soon to be 5-year-old's question reveals an important insight: Everywhere we look, we see the same letters, not an endless variety of forms.

Continuing Use of Scribbles, Mock Letters, and Actual Letters

Once children have attained the insight that there are a limited rather than an end-less number of letters, mock letters seldom appear in their writing, except during play. When children make props for play scenarios, they generally recognize that the props are "just pretend" and that written marks needn't be "real" letters. Writ-ing for this purpose, even among 5-year-olds, may be a combination of scribbles, mock letters, and actual letters. More often, though, we see actual letters, or good approximations to them, combined with scribble writing, which is easier and faster to produce than are mock or actual letters. We see just this combination of marks on a ticket a child prepared for a classroom production of *The Three Little Pigs* (see Figure 5.5). Notice that the forms at the top of the ticket are the numerals 1 through 10.

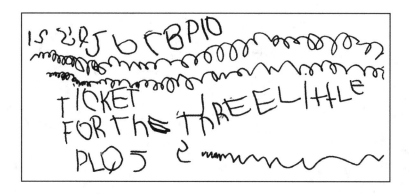

FIGURE 5.5. Ticket for *The Three Little Pigs*.

In nonplay situations, older 4-year-old and younger 5-year-old children typically use forms that are actual letters, although their skill in creating them is limited in many ways. Consider the samples provided in Figure 5.6. Figure 5.6a comes from a sign-up sheet provided in a block area. When the block area was full (occupants were limited to four at a time), children who wanted turns wrote their names on a sheet of paper attached to a clipboard. The name at the top of this list is *SARAH*. She started in the middle of the paper with the letter *S*, wrote the letters *A* and *R*, and then ran out of room. She returned to the middle of the paper and wrote *A* to the left of *S*, then added *H* to the left of that. For Sarah, budding knowledge of directionality collided with the challenge of available space.

Sarah's print placement strategies are very typical among preschoolers. She started in a place that did not give her enough space to write all of a word on one line. Then she fit in the rest of the letters as best she could. Sometimes, children rotate the paper and write the remaining letters on what first had been the right side of the paper, but ends up, at least for a time, as the top.

Notice that Sarah knew the letters of her name, wrote them in the correct temporal order, and started out writing from left to right. Had Sarah started at the left-hand margin (rather than in the middle of the page), she might have returned to the left to finish writing. But there was space, right there on the original line, so why not fill it?

Had Sarah's teacher not observed her, she might have drawn the conclusion that Sarah started with *H* and went from there, jumbling the order of the letters in her name. Not so. Sarah did not yet know that she should always sweep to the left and write the remaining letters from left to right under her top row.

A similar dilemma caused a different child to resist her teacher's suggestion that she put the *A* that follows *R* in the word *library* under the *L* she had written in the first line (see Figure 5.6b). She wanted the *R* and *A* to be "together," she explained, "because they come together in the word." While children have their reasons for doing things, gradually they begin to see things as adults see them.

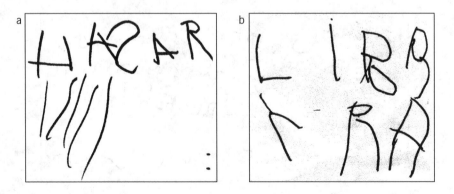

FIGURE 5.6. Use of actual alphabet letters.

They realize that abiding by conventions allows others to interpret their writing. In the meantime, teachers can enjoy preschoolers' efforts and accept some of their thoughtful accommodations to the challenges they encounter.

A Close Look at the Letters Preschoolers Create

Even when they have accepted that the finite set of alphabet symbols should be used for writing, preschoolers form letters in interesting ways. Notice that in Figure 5.6a Sarah reversed the *S* in her name. *S* is a difficult letter for young children to orient correctly because making the first move in the wrong direction reverses the letter. Notice that the only other curved line in Sarah's name is in the upper portion of *R* and that the movement for this curved line starts in the opposite direction needed to write *S*.

Reversed letters are very common in the writing of preschool and kindergarten children. In most cases, there is no confusion about which letter they have written; for preschoolers, orientation appears not to matter. Teachers can support children's acquisition of knowledge about letter orientation by commenting, for example, that, "*M* and *W* are just alike, except one faces up and the other faces down." For older preschoolers, teachers might contrast the direction of movement when making *S* and *2* in quick demonstrations provided at the writing table, as appropriate to the children's current endeavors. When working with a group of children on shared writing, a teacher also might comment, when starting the letter *S*, "I start here and then go this way, and then back around like this. If I go the other way, my *S* will be backward. We would still know that it is *S*, but I want my *S* to go the way it is supposed to go."

We also see a lot of imprecision in the marks that preschoolers use to compose other alphabet letters. Notice the *B* in *library* in Figure 5.6b. The child did splendidly with the top closed curve but had some difficulty with the bottom portion. (It is possible she thought *P* at first, and then repaired it to form a *B*, but we cannot be certain.) The *R*'s in *library* are also interesting. The diagonal line that makes up the lower right half of *R* caused the child some trouble. Diagonal lines are often difficult for children in preschool, in part because children need to control where the line should begin and project where it must end. It should be apparent, then, that learning to properly form alphabet letters is not a matter of simply copying letter forms. Whether determining how many horizontal lines there are in an uppercase *E* versus *F*, or knowing how many diagonal lines intersect the curved line of a *Q*— and where the diagonal should go—children must keep lots of information in mind as they begin to write using conventional alphabet letters. Few preschoolers will be able to master the ability to write the full set of upper- and lowercase letters, properly formed and correctly oriented. The goal should be to ensure that children recognize as many letters as possible and feel comfortable using them as best they can to convey meaning.

As described here, then, the journey from scribbles to script involves three major discoveries. First, children must become aware of the differences in the marks used to make pictures as opposed to print. Then, they must recognize that the lines of print they create are actually comprised of individual symbols composed with both straight and curved lines. Finally, they must discover that there is a finite set of alphabet letters and learn how to form each of those. The other journey they must take entails deciding which of these letters they should use to create the words they want to use. This journey moves them from creation of mock words to writing of real words using alphabetic spelling.

THE JOURNEY FROM MOCK WORDS TO ALPHABETIC SPELLING

Just as preschool children develop their skill in creating marks and forming letters, they also develop skill using letters first to approximate and then to create actual words. Beginning at approximately age 3, once children are making mock letters and rudimentary approximations of some actual letters, they begin to put their letter-like designs together to make "words." These mock words (made-up creations that look like words, but are not) are initially comprised of letter strings, groupings of letters that are used to represent words with no consideration of letter sounds. They make considerable progress in developing a beginning understanding of word making throughout the rest of their preschool years.

Children very slowly begin to grasp the pivotal importance of the selection of specific letters and their sequencing in written communication as they develop phonological awareness, learn letter names, and observe their teacher's demonstrations of breaking spoken words into their individual sounds and linking these to the letter or letters that represent them. Children also learn more about word making as they talk about their writing with teachers, and as they observe and interact with the print that surrounds them.

We know, however, that simply immersing children in a print-rich environment is not enough. Children "read" the entire physical context that surrounds environmental print, to determine what it "says" or means, without looking much at the print itself (Masonheimer, Drum, & Ehri, 1984; Reutzel, Fawson, Young, Morrison, & Wilcox, 2003). This is why it is important to engage preschoolers in other activities in which the code-based nature of print is made more obvious.

At first, preschoolers have no understanding that print is mapped onto oral language. Their experimentation with word creation is more visual, with environmental print serving as an important source of knowledge about how words look, though not of why each word looks exactly as it does—why those letters, in that order. Even after children acquire the basic insight that print and speech are related, the precise way in which they are related eludes them. Only gradually do preschoolers begin to realize that letters represent the individual sounds in spoken words. This realization is furthered by strategies like those shared in Chapter 4 that are designed to help children develop phonemic awareness and alphabetic knowledge.

Skill in accurately isolating all the sounds in words and knowing which letters represent them are beyond the capability of most preschoolers, especially younger ones. With older 4-year-olds, however, we often do see the beginnings of an under-standing of the basic processes involved in conventional word making. Our com-prehension of how children develop this understanding is based on pioneering, sys-tematic work by Baghban (1984), Clay (1975, 1987), and Invernizzi (2003), and on the countless contributions of others who have studied young children's writing.

Use of Environmental Print

As we described in Chapter 2, children are surrounded by environmental print, both in and outside of school. Imagine all the products with printed labels that children see in their homes on a daily basis—their toothpaste, cereal, milk car-tons, and snack containers. On their way to school, children see street signs and the print on the fronts of commercial establishments. The latter include fast food outlets and grocery stores with words that they may already "read" when they see them in context. When taken out of context, though, preschoolers typically can-not read words that they have seen many times, and "read" in their typical context (Reutzel et al., 2003). Preschool classrooms offer even more environmental print, most of it actively created and used by the children and the teachers (see Figure 5.7). As children and teachers work together with the print that surrounds them every day, it becomes a tool for children's learning.

When children inspect print that is all around them, they notice, for example, that words usually consist of more than one letter, and create mock words that typically contain three to seven letters—the typical range of letters in the words they see in their environment. They also recognize that words contain a variety of letters, and therefore rarely create mock words by repeating just one letter three or four times. They also realize that the same letters appear in many different words and that the very same letters can be used to make different words, if the letters are reordered. Their mock words reflect these insights. Children also sometimes use letters from familiar words, especially their own names and those of their classmates, as a base from which to form new mock words, and they also "bor-row" whole words from environmental print to create their own messages, often without regard for what the words actually say (Fields, 1998; Invernizzi, 2003). Sometimes, children simply want to create print artifacts, and because in these cases there is no specific message being conveyed anyway, any "words" will work.

The writing in Figure 5.8 illustrates the variety of ways children incorporate environmental print into their own creations. After visiting an aquarium as part of their investigation of ocean life, these 4-year-olds were invited to draw their

FIGURE 5.7. Preschool classroom environmental print.

FIGURE 5.8. Influence of environmental print on children's writing.

favorite ocean animals on paper cut out to resemble fish bowls. The teacher modeled the activity, labeling her own drawings with the words *shark*, *octopus*, and *eel*. Some children produced drawings but did not label them. The only print on their papers was their own name. Some children used classmates' names in their drawings and writing, confidently asserting that those were the names of the different fish, an example of borrowing environmental print without regard for its meaning. Notice that one child did not draw any fish, but filled her bowl with print—some copied from a list of classmates' names, and one word, *pizza*, copied twice from a chart created as a shared writing activity during which children listed their favorite pizza toppings. It seems that this child just wanted to create words, and copied some from the environment. Two children created their own "words" in addition to copying names and other words. Note that not a single child demonstrated understanding of the alphabetic principle—that to form words, we must select letters that represent the specific sounds in a spoken word. The absence of this insight is quite typical among preschool children.

The individual variations in the children's performances also illustrate how preschoolers often stray from a teacher's assignment to engage in drawing and writing. Their teacher accepted each child's creation, knowing that motivation to write and draw comes from having considerable control over what and when to do one or the other, or both. It is probably worthwhile for preschool teachers occasionally to model and suggest specific things that children might do. Preschoolers then need freedom to take things in the direction they wish.

Children's Names as a Special Source of Knowledge about Word Making

We saw in Figure 5.8 that children's names are often prominent in their writing and drawing. In fact, as discussed in Chapter 4, children probably first become aware of both letters and words through engagement with their names. We know that the first letters a child is likely to learn are those from their names (Cabell et al., 2013; Treiman & Broderick, 1998; Treiman, Cohen, Mulqueeny, Kessler, & Schechtman, 2007). As we see in Figure 5.9, pictures and letter shapes are often equally prominent in a child's earliest attempts to use letters to convey specific meanings. This sample was produced by 4-year-old Brianna in a post office dramatic play center. Together, the pictures and letters constituted a letter to her aunt. When her teacher asked what the letter said, Brianna read, "Dear Auntie Shante, I am coming to see you. Me and Mommy and Henry. We coming. Love, Brianna."

For Brianna, meaning was represented as much by the picture as by the print, and she relied on oral language to explain both pictures and letters. The important thing to know about the letters was that almost all were from her name. She indicated that the *NA* at the bottom of the page said "love Brianna." Apparently, Brianna knew that letters were needed to write the rest of her message to her aunt.

FIGURE 5.9. Children's names influence their writing.

She borrowed letters from her name, no doubt because they were those she knew best how to write. Brianna's willingness to reuse letters from her name to create other "words" (mock ones, to be sure) demonstrates a budding understanding that letters in her name also can be used in other words.

Billy, a classmate of Brianna, had also shown a lot of interest in his name. He could spell it aloud, letter by letter, and he tried to write it, too, although he wasn't always able to write each letter as he recited it. Billy wrote a letter to his older brother, Odell, who had gone on a trip with their father. Figure 5.10 shows that Billy used variations of his name, over and over again, to complete his letter. He read it to his teacher as follows: "Odell, I been missing you. Come home tomorrow. Love, Billy. Come home now."

While still relying on his name as the basic source of letters to write to his brother, Billy nonetheless demonstrated a more sophisticated understanding of writing than did Brianna. For example, he reused letters in his name and altered their sequence in his name to create other "words." Apparently, he had observed that the same letters can be used to spell many different words and that some words differ by only one letter (e.g., *cake* and *Coke*, *Mike* and *Ike*). In many cases Billy added just one new mark to *Billy* (e.g., *Billly*, *BiClly*, and *Belly*). In *Belly*, the addition of a letter *e* substituted for the letter that occupies that spot in his name (*i*). In one "word," Billy used a second strategy: recombining letters in a new sequence (*BilBi*). He also used a third strategy: deleting letters to create a shorter "word" (*Bil*).

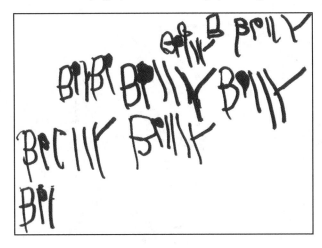

FIGURE 5.10. Variations of names for writing.

As children begin to move beyond relying on the letters in their names to create new "words," their awareness of general visual characteristics of words, obtained from observation of environmental print, frequently leads them to produce mock words comprised of many more letters. These strings of letters certainly look like real words, even though their letters do not represent the sound sequences of actual words in our language.

In this phase of stringing letters together to create words, without any knowledge of the need to select and order letters to represent the order of sounds heard in spoken words, children have not yet discovered how print works in English and other alphabetic languages. Until they develop the alphabetic principle, they do not understand that letters represent sounds. Their intention is to make their writing look like it is composed of words, and they believe at first that the mock words they create are actual words.

The writing sample in Figure 5.11 was produced by 5-year-old Marisol in her preschool classroom's writing center. According to Marisol, her writing says, "I like my dog. I take good care of him." Her writing, like Billy's, uses nonphonemic letter strings—letters arranged in a string, but not selected and sequenced to match the sound structure of an actual word. Unlike Billy, however, Marisol uses many letters, not just those drawn mostly from her name. In fact, there are 11 distinct letters among the 25 symbols she created in this sample. Her writing looks a lot more like "real" writing than Billy's because she has written many more different "words," given her larger repertoire of letters to use.

Children typically continue this kind of exploration for months until they finally realize that this approach doesn't work very well for making actual words. They then begin to ask their teacher for spellings, they copy words from the environment, or they ask other adults for correct spellings.

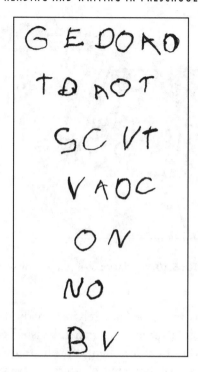

FIGURE 5.11. Creation of mock words for writing.

Beginnings of Phonemic Spelling

A major developmental leap in writing occurs when children discover that spoken words are made up of sounds, and that these have some connection to letters in printed words. A beginning awareness of the sounds in words is first demonstrated when children begin to divide words into syllables, and syllables into onsets (all of the sounds prior to the first vowel, such as /b/ in *boy* and /str/ in *string*) and rimes (the vowel and all that follows, such as /oy/ in /b/-/oy/, and /ing/ in /str/-/ing/). These levels of phonological processing precede phonemic awareness, which is awareness of individual sounds in words, not awareness of larger chunks, such as syllables or onset-rime units. Phonemic awareness develops gradually as children are engaged in experiences that bring these smaller units of sound in words to their attention.

During the preschool years, beginning levels of phonological awareness develop as children engage in language play such as play with rhyming words and words that begin with the same sound (i.e., alliteration) as we described in Chapter 4. Experiences like singing songs that play with language provide a level of support (scaffolding) that enables children to successfully manipulate sounds as they sing along, even though they are not likely at first to be skilled in isolating and manipulating phonemes on their own. Repeated engagement in this type of playful activity, as well as others, leads over time to growth in phonological awareness.

Preschool teachers can enhance children's phonemic-level awareness by reciting poems with a lot of alliteration and then talking about the words that begin with the same sound, after a poem has been recited. Teachers can also engage children in playing games like "I Spy," in which children are encouraged to find objects in the classroom that begin with particular sounds. For example, a teacher might say, "I spy something that starts with /m/, like Marisol's name . . . /m/ *Marisol*. I want you to think about objects in our classroom and decide whether any of them have names that start with /m/." To participate, children must say the names of objects they see or know about and then isolate the first sound of an object's name. They must then match it to /m/, the target sound the teacher has provided. As you can see, this activity requires children to isolate the individual sound—the phoneme—at the beginning of a word.

It is also the case, however, that isolating an initial sound in a word when a single-consonant phoneme constitutes all of a syllable's onset (e.g., *b-oy*, *d-og*) is much easier for children to detect than is isolating the first phoneme of an onset that is a consonant cluster (e.g., /s/ in *str*, which is the onset of *string*), or to separate the individual sounds in a syllable's rime unit (e.g., /k/ separated from *ack*, the rime unit in *black*) (Treiman, 1985).

Still, the practice of isolating the first sound in words with a single-consonant phoneme is worthwhile for children, and it is most beneficial to their writing when paired with writing the letter that represents the sound isolated. In this way, children learn letter names, as a teacher says, "That's right. The first sound we hear in the word *bird* is /b/. We use the letter *B* to write /b/, so I will write that letter, right here." They also learn the alphabetic principle (i.e., letters function to represent sounds in spoken words) and some specific sound–letter matches.

Connecting letters to specific sounds is not a simple task for preschoolers. To do this, they must distinguish among letter shapes and know each letter's name, and must know that letters are used to write sounds we hear in words (i.e., understand the alphabetic principle). Many young children can recognize and name all the letters of the alphabet but have no idea how to use them to make words. As a consequence, they continue to create mock words by stringing letters together because they have no idea how letters are actually used to make words.

Teachers can help children understand the alphabetic principle if they demonstrate writing by sounding out words and then represent each sound with a letter or letters. This thinking out loud as the teacher writes can be done as a natural part of preschool classroom routines.

A teacher might say, for example, when involving children in making labels for art center supplies, "This sign is for the markers. Let's see, /m/, /m/, /m/, /m/ . . . *markers*. The word *markers* starts with the letter *m*, so I'll write the *m* first, right here." The teacher might then say, "I hear /r/ next, but I know there's an *a* before it that we don't hear, so I will write that first and then write *r* for /r/. Then, I hear /k/, mark /k/, so I'll write *k* next. . . ." By transcribing a spoken word into its written form, the teacher explicitly models the most fundamental of literacy concepts—the fact that print conveys meaning—and also precisely how print works to represent meaning in languages with alphabetic writing systems. Such an authentic use of print serves many important literacy purposes—and also serves the social purpose of helping to keep the art center neat.

Preschool teachers will also want to label children's drawings or paintings after talking with children about them. Here, again, the teacher can think aloud the spelling of some of the most prominent words as they are written. A teacher has yet another opportunity when a child "anchors" a message in scribble writing and then approaches the teacher to talk about it. If the child is agreeable, and if it serves the child's purposes, the teacher can help in writing some actual words to go with the scribble the child has created. Perhaps the child would like the teacher to write "Dear Mommy" or some other part of the message. Using the highly informative think-aloud strategy the teacher can help the child. All of these activities— songs, teacher-demonstrated writing, individual writing assistance, and practice games, introduced to the whole group and then put out in learning centers—help children develop phonological awareness, letter name knowledge, the alphabetic principle, and some specific sound–letter connections.

When children begin to understand the way that sounds are connected to letters from having seen teachers demonstrate these connections, they often begin to create phonemic-based spellings on their own. Sometimes, this occurs while they are still writing letters that are not very conventional. Four-year-old Helen demonstrated her budding phonemic awareness and sound–letter connections in the message shown in Figure 5.12, which she created for her best friend, Cameron. She explained to her teacher that the print on the left says, "I love Cameron." When

FIGURE 5.12. Beginning alphabet writing.

asked about the symbols on the right side of the page, she pointed out the hearts and indicated that those show how much she loves her friend. Then she said, the rest of the writing says, "I want you to play at my house."

Helen's representation of just two of the three sounds in a word is typical of children who first begin to use phonemic spelling. The /l/ and /v/ are dominant sounds in the word *love*, and are also the first and last sounds, which are easiest for children to focus on. The middle phoneme in *love*, a vowel, is harder for children to detect.

CM for *Cameron* is also an interesting example of abbreviated word making. The second phoneme in *Cameron* is a soft vowel, which is relatively hard to hear. Helen did not represent any of the sounds in the second and third syllables of Cameron's name. Since the first syllable of Cameron's name is the one accented, it is likely that Helen was not as aware of the sounds in the unaccented syllables that followed. Often, children only represent the most obvious sounds they hear in words, and also include just enough to satisfy their intent of writing the word. Even if Helen had heard some of the sounds in the last two syllables of Cameron's name, she might have decided it wasn't necessary to represent them.

Children do not immediately abandon earlier forms of word making when they first create some phonemic-based spellings. We can see Helen's use of scribbled symbols in the second part of her message. Figure 5.13 likewise illustrates that even older preschool children mix writing forms. Five-year-old Jackson read this journal entry as "My mom fixes me spinach and turkey and gravy. It is good." This appears at first glance to be a mix of letter string words and scribble writing. Closer examination, however, reveals that Jackson engaged in significant phonemic spelling. The *mi* on the first line may represent *my*, while the *fes* is for *fixes*.

FIGURE 5.13. Alphabetic and scribble writing mixed.

The word *me* is represented with a single letter *m*, and *spinach* is spelled *snh*, representing the three major consonant sounds in the word. The name of the letter *H* contains /aich/, which explains his selection of that letter as the last in spinach. Use of this letter-name strategy is also evident in children's use of single letters to represent entire words, as when they write *C* for *see*, *R* for *are*, and *U* for *you*. In these cases, the letter names have in them the sequence of two sounds heard in these words.

The letter strings and scribble that follow the first two lines in Jackson's message suggest that he wanted to create lots of writing but couldn't sustain the level of effort needed to continue sounding out words and selecting letters. It is very common for preschoolers to tire as they write messages and resort to other forms that remain in their repertoire.

Movement along a Developmental Continuum

Once children fully understand that writing involves organizing letters into clusters based on the sound sequence in words, they follow a very common progression from representing only the most prominent sounds in words to representing most of the sounds they hear. Most preschool children are only able to represent most or all of the sounds in words if they have significant support. Moreover, regardless of the extent to which all children in a class participate in the same activities, they will develop the ability to produce phonemic spelling at different rates. Figure 5.14 illustrates the variation in the spelling skills of a group of preschoolers in the same classroom at the end of the year before they were to enter kindergarten. After the teacher demonstrated spelling four words, sounding out and representing each sound with a single letter, children could then select a picture to paste onto the poster and write a label for it. The teacher assisted children by slowly enunciating each child's word. Some children were able to represent all of the phonemes in their words, while others represented only beginning and ending consonants. Some children showed more control than others over letter formation, although fine motor control did not seem to be related to the child's ability to match letters to sounds.

Preschool children rarely move beyond the beginning stages of phoneme-based spelling. Many will reach that phase of spelling in kindergarten; others not until first grade. If preschool teachers are aware of the full progression of word-creation development, they can support the continued growth of all children in their classrooms, wherever they fall on the developmental continuum. If teachers know what kind of word-creation strategy a child is likely to use next, they can plan activities and interact with individual children in ways that nudge them toward the next level for them.

The samples in this chapter illustrate how much preschoolers learn about using written language, and how much is left for most of them to learn as they continue on in kindergarten (and beyond). They first attempt to write words by using the

FIGURE 5.14. Variations of spelling ability in one preschool classroom.

letters in their names and copying letters and words from the environment. Until children figure out that letters are mapped to speech, their "words" are mock letter strings that look like words but are not. As children realize that sounds in words are represented by letters, they begin to attempt phoneme-based spellings, but first represent very few of the sounds in a word, often only the first. Gradually, they begin to isolate more sounds in words and include more and more letters in the words they try to write. Eventually, and usually not until they are in kindergarten or first grade, children represent most of the sounds that actually make up a word they try to spell.

Teachers can help children by offering opportunities for them to play with language, to explore letters and sounds, and to experiment with writing. Shared writing is an integrated strategy that engages children and teachers in the writing process together.

SHARED WRITING: ANOTHER INTEGRATED INSTRUCTIONAL STRATEGY

When engaging children in shared writing, the teacher models the writing process as students observe or participate and respond. Shared writing is a process that can be used in many contexts, whether to create meaningful morning messages, to record children's observations from explorations of concepts in centers, or to consolidate children's comprehension of books they have read (Gerde, Bingham, & Wasik, 2012; Strickland & Riley-Ayers, 2006).

What Shared Writing Does

Shared writing allows the teacher, a skilled writer, to guide children from thinking and talking to writing. As the teacher thinks aloud about what will be written and how it will be spelled, children witness the way letters, sounds, and words are linked to express ideas in written form. The teacher demonstrates the conventions of print by noting when children need to use a capital letter or a period, for example. Of course, very young children are not expected to know all of this, but they do gain familiarity with the language of literacy: the letter *m*, the end of a word, the beginning of a new sentence, and so on. Shared writing gradually moves to more interactive writing in which the children are encouraged and expected to participate. This progression helps children gain familiarity with the writing process.

How to Do Shared Writing

Step 1

Start with an inquiry activity in which children are engaged in experiences of interest and importance to them. This may be a hands-on activity, such as planting seeds or caring for a pet, or it may be a literature-based activity, such as a discussion of a book that has been read aloud. Experiences such as these spark children's interest and stimulate language and thinking.

Step 2

Guide children in a discussion about the activity they have experienced or the material they have heard you read. Decide which ideas should be written down, and say to the children, "We can save these ideas by writing them down."

Step 3

Do a "write-aloud" to model or demonstrate for the children. During a write-aloud, you think aloud as you write, as if you were talking to yourself. For example, say, "Let me see, I think that I will write down the things I need to plant the seeds. I will need some soil. *Soil* starts with /s/, and we use the letter *s* to stand for /s/. So, I will write the letter *s* first. I know that the other letters are *o, i,* and *l, s-o-i-l: soil.*" Finish writing the word *soil* and follow the same process to write the other words you will need. The amount written may be several sentences or only one or two words.

If you wish to involve the children in more interactive shared writing, you might pause at points along the way where you think they might be able to participate. For example, you might say, "I know that the word *soil* starts with /s/, just like Sandra's name. Sandra, do you think you know what letter I need?" Or you might simply wish to have the children call out what they think the letter will be without you offering a word to link it to.

Figure 5.15 shows one group's shared writing composition. In this example, children's responses to *If You Give a Mouse a Cookie* by Laura Joffe Numeroff (1985) include oral and written language as well as a hands-on activity. Their words and actions are captured through print and then illustrated with photos.

Step 4

A shared writing chart may be completed in one day or in brief segments over a period of several days. When the chart is complete or when the children have done

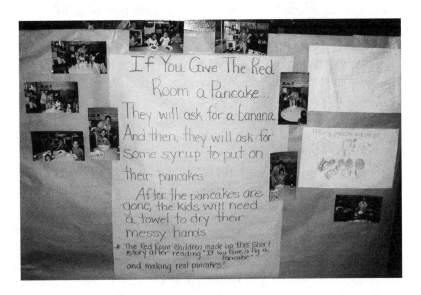

FIGURE 5.15. Shared writing in response to literature.

enough for one sitting, guide them in a reading of what has been written. Children can "read" along to the best of their ability. If the writing occurs over several days, it is a good idea to start each new session by rereading what has already been written. This helps reorient the children to the task and their purpose for writing. Then, continue with the new writing and end with a complete rereading of everything.

Step 5

Rereading may be followed by a guided discussion of the things children notice about the text. Point to the words and say, for example, "I notice that the word *soil* and the word *seeds* both start with the same letter. That letter is *s*. Does anyone else notice anything they would like to tell us about? Can anyone find the letter *s* somewhere else?" You may have to model this "noticing" process for several weeks before the children catch on. Keep it brief and expect that many children will gradually begin "noticing" with you.

Step 6

Be sure to place the completed chart where it is accessible to children for independent examination and additional writing during periods of free play.

Step 7

Use independent drawing or writing as a follow-up activity for those children who are interested. These compositions may be shared with the class, if the children are willing.

The following list summarizes the ways that teachers can model literacy behaviors and encourage children's involvement during shared writing to support their development of print concepts. The teacher:

- Involves children in an activity or discussion that generates a shared experience worth writing about.
- Acts as scribe (at the chalkboard, on a smart board, or on a chart).
- Thinks aloud about content and language.
- Speaks and comments while writing.
- Pauses for children to suggest words or letters that might come next.
- Guides group reading and rereading.
- Guides the analysis of text by discussing ideas and noticing print language patterns (e.g., repeated phrases) and known elements (e.g., letters and words).

- Encourages children to "try out" reading the chart on their own.
- Encourages children to "try out" writing on their own and provides materials and guidance at their request.

Variations and Extensions

Shared writing does not have to be limited to whole-class creation of charts. Teachers can also help children develop alphabetic knowledge for writing through a combination of whole-class activities and direct small-group instruction, such as dictated or shared writing in which sounding out spoken words to spell them is demonstrated. Within the groups, individual children can be given more extensive practice with various aspects of writing.

Stepping Up to Write

When the shared writing chart is completed, invite individual children to "step up" (McGee, 2007) to work with the print. They may, for example, find and circle a specific letter that they are studying that week. Or perhaps they can find and underline a word that begins with a particular letter or that is repeated many times. They may be invited to copy any word or letter from the chart on white space at the bottom. Have no more than three or four children step up. Then, place the chart where it is accessible to children and remind them that they can read and write on the chart during center time. Figure 5.16 shows a group of children writing independently on a shared writing chart during free play in their classroom. The circling and underlining on the chart are the result of children "stepping up" during the shared writing activity.

Creating a Daily Class Journal

Many teachers keep a class journal in which individual children or the whole class dictates a sentence or two each day. At the end of each week, the teacher punches holes in the new pages so they can be placed with other pages in a class journal bound by three metal rings. Some teachers leave space on each page for children's illustrations. The pages of the class journal may be laminated, and the journal may be placed in the library center, where children can enjoy it as a read-aloud or explore it during independent reading time.

Alternately, the class journal can be created as an e-book using one of any number of book creation apps available for tablets or smart boards. The teacher can write children's dictated messages onto each page, perhaps using a think-aloud process as children watch. The resulting e-books can be stored on classroom devices accessible to the children for later rereading and also sent electronically to parents via built-in sharing functions common to most of these apps.

FIGURE 5.16. Writing on shared writing chart during center activity.

Varying the Forms of and Purposes of Writing

It is important that children are exposed over time to a variety of forms and purposes for writing. Children's names, lists, instructions, informal notes, and labels needed in the room are all good content for shared writing. These can be created with the whole class, in small groups, or with individual children.

Scaffolding the Activity for Developmental Appropriateness

Shared writing activities should be adjusted in length and with respect to vocabulary use according to the ages, maturity levels, and skills of the children. Also vary the amount of support that is offered as children engage in these activities. For example, some children may be able to step up and find a specific letter by simply scanning the entire chart. Others may need to be directed to a single line that contains the letter. Still others may need to be directed to a single line or even a single word while also viewing a plastic magnetic letter to help them remember the form of the letter they are looking for. In preschool, children's interest in whole-class activities typically wanes after 15 minutes or so of sustained attention. Limit the whole-class activity to a relatively brief period of time, but be sure to remind children that the materials will be available for them to explore on their own as a center activity.

How to Accommodate Differences

Accommodations for English Language Learners

Young English language learners must hear and see their own language represented in instructional activities if they are to discern the connection between oral language and print (Fitzgerald & Amendum, 2007). Include in shared writing activities some words in children's first languages other than English whenever feasible. You may need to ask others for spelling assistance, but it is worth the extra effort to demonstrate that other languages are valued and that they too can be written down.

Allow children to dictate individual pages for class journals in whatever language they choose. Recording the child's dictated message, either using the recording function built into e-book creation apps, or with the memo-recording function included on most smartphones, will facilitate this process. If the language is unfamiliar to the teacher, he or she can share the recording with a parent or someone else who speaks the language to find out how to write the message with conventional spelling and punctuation. The recordings can also be used with voice-to-text or translation programs, although those may not be accurate given preschool children's often immature pronunciations of words even in their native tongues.

Accommodations for Atypical Learners

In any group, the children will vary widely in their understanding of what you are attempting to convey through shared writing. At the very least, children need to understand that their thoughts and speech can be written down and that people use letters to form words in order to do this. These fundamental concepts of print underlie the more refined concepts children need to learn in order to read and write. Focus on these big ideas with children who are developing more slowly than others, and then build to more complex concepts.

Accommodations for Advanced Learners

Children who show an interest in independent drawing and writing should be gently guided through the following writing process as they attempt to write on their own.

- *Prewriting*: Help children discuss ideas they want to draw or write about.
- *Drafting*: Encourage children to draw about their ideas and write something to accompany their drawings. Encourage them to use what they know about letters and sounds as they write. Follow the children's lead. Offer assistance if you hear a child attempting to sound out a word, perhaps by repeating it softly, stretching out the sounds. Answer children's questions about spelling but avoid pushing them beyond their interest or ability levels.
- *Revising*: When a child is finished drawing or writing, ask, "Is your picture/ story just the way you want it to be?" Get children in the habit of looking over what they have done. Most often they will say it is fine. Now and then, they may want to add something.
- *Sharing*: During sharing time, invite children to talk about their pictures and "read" what they have written. Children may share individual writing with the teacher, individual peers, or the whole class.

This process may be used with all children. However, it is important to follow the child's lead and provide instruction according to each child's needs.

FOCUSED STRATEGIES FOR SHARED WRITING

The strategies in this section are designed to focus children's attention on specific concepts about print. The variations described for broader shared writing can also be used for these focused strategies.

Focused Strategy 1: Things I Like

Children collect pictures of things they like, such as food, toys, or hobbies. These are pasted on paper and labeled by the teacher as children watch.

What It Does

This strategy supports children's understanding that speech can be written down and supports their development of concept of word and concept of letter.

How to Do It

You will need old magazines, scissors, glue or paste, and 8½″ × 11″ pieces of paper.

Step 1. Provide a generous supply of pictures cut from magazines or other sources. You will need at least three or four per child.

Step 2. Print the words "Things I Like" at the top of a large piece of paper for each child. Ask the children to choose three pictures of things they like. Assist them in pasting the pictures on the paper.

Step 3. Have each child name aloud each item in the pictures he or she selected. Write the name of each item next to its picture, saying aloud the letters as you write.

Step 4. When the writing is complete, read the words again, pointing to each word and encouraging the child to join in.

Variations

Varying the Theme. You may wish to change the theme of the picture collection (e.g., "Toys I Like" or "Animals I Like").

Finding a Word. When the writing is complete, use a separate sheet of paper to write down one of the words. Ask the child to find that word on his or her paper.

Finding a Letter. When the writing is complete, use a separate sheet of paper to write down a letter from one of the words. Name the letter and ask the child to find that letter in other words.

How to Accommodate Differences

Accommodations for English Language Learners. Whenever possible, inquire about what something is called in the language the child speaks at home and write the word in both English and the child's home language. If you are unsure of how the word is spelled in the child's home language, simply have the child say the word for you and do not attempt to write it.

Accommodations for Atypical Learners. For the child who is developing more slowly than most, point out how symbols stand for things. For example, touch the chair the child is sitting on and say, "This is a real chair that you are sitting on right now." Show a picture of a chair and say, "Here is a picture of a chair." Write the word *chair* and say, "This is the word that stands for chair, and we can read it and write it. This is the word *chair.*"

Accommodations for Advanced Learners. After writing a word, you might ask, "Do you see any letters you know?" Say a word and then ask, "Can you tell me how that word sounds at the very beginning?" Choose only the beginning sounds that you think the child might be familiar with, and provide plenty of support.

Focused Strategy 2: Room Word Search

This strategy requires children to search for and copy particular words in the classroom. It will help solidify their concept of word and prompt them to attend to the individual letters that comprise the word.

What It Does

Engaging children in a room word search encourages them to notice the environmental print around them and offers them an opportunity to discuss the words and their uses in the classroom.

How to Do It

Step 1. This might be the final activity during whole-class time. Say to the children, "I am going to show you a word that is somewhere in this room. It is the word *crayons*. I will spell it." Point to the letters in the word as you say them and then say the word once again. Ask, "Who would like to see if they can find the word?" Use meaning prompts to help them think critically: "Where do you think the word *crayons* might be found in our classroom?"

Step 2. Provide clipboards with blank paper for all children. Select two children, give them a copy of the word, and ask them to search for another example of the word somewhere in the room. When they have found the word, all the other children may gather around to see if it is the correct choice. Ask, "Are the two words the same?" Then say, "Let's look closely and spell it again. Let's look at the first letter. It is the letter *c*. Do both words start with the letter *c*?" Continue with the other letters until everyone agrees that the words are the same, not different. Use the terms *same* and *different* whenever possible because these words are constantly used in literacy instruction.

Step 3. Invite the children to copy the word onto their individual papers. Note that not all children will be able to copy the word accurately. Accuracy and correct letter formation matter less than children's careful attention to the individual letters in the word.

Step 4. Repeat this process with one or two more words, giving other children a chance to lead the search.

Step 5. When appropriate, talk about how the chosen word is useful in the classroom: "The word *crayons* helps us know that our crayons are kept in this tub."

Step 6. Place those and other words in a bin in the writing center and encourage children to search for them independently during their free play if they choose.

Variations

Using Small Groups. After demonstrating the activity with the whole class, you might want to work with only two or three children each day, allowing sufficient time to engage them in extended conversation.

Searching Charts or Big Books. Have children search for words on a chart that the class has created or in a Big Book that has been read aloud several times.

How to Accommodate Differences

Accommodations for English Language Learners. In cases where you have labels written in two languages, use one or the other, and identify the language for the children. State and spell the word and say, "See if you can find it."

Accommodations for Atypical Learners. Choose very obvious words for children who are just beginning to get the idea that the same word can be written down in more than one place. Stress how the words function in the classroom. Use words that have meaning for the child, such as familiar names, labels in the room, and words that have appeared over and over again in charts created through shared writing. Too often, learning is made very rote for these children and lacks an appreciation that all children need meaningful opportunities to develop genuine understanding.

Accommodations for Advanced Learners. Some children will have already demonstrated an interest in the words in the environment by asking questions about them and attempting to read them on their own. Use the room word search similarly with them, but ask them to try it without taking the word card with them unless they need it. After they think they have found the word, they may use the word card to double-check it. This is a good visual memory activity.

Focused Strategy 3: Building Words

This strategy requires children to reconstruct familiar words, phrases, and sentences. After this activity is modeled with the whole group, the materials may be placed in a learning center where children can do the activity individually or in pairs.

What It Does

This strategy requires that children look at parts within a whole. They learn that word and letter orders are important and that English words and letters are arranged from left to right.

How to Do It

Step 1. You will need two identical copies of the words, phrases, or very short sentences you plan to use. One copy should be left as is to serve as a model; the other should be cut into letters or words. Place all the pieces in a plastic bag.

Step 2. Have children dump out the contents of the bag and attempt to reconstruct the cut-up pieces to match the model copy.

Step 3. Children should only work with words, phrases, and sentences with which they are very familiar. For example, you might select a word that is repeated several times on a class chart. After repeated readings of a Big Book with patterned text, select a short phrase or sentence that the children have joined in to read along with you. For example, use "I think I can," "Jump, Frog, Jump!" or "He was still hungry."

Variations

Using Child-Created Sentences. Ask a child to dictate a sentence. Write it down and make a duplicate copy. Cut out one copy and have the child reconstruct the sentence he or she has dictated. This variation introduces the idea that each printed word stands for a spoken word. Children will also begin to see that printed words have spaces between them, unlike spoken words, which run together as people say them aloud.

How to Accommodate Differences

Accommodations for English Language Learners. This activity can be done in any language. When demonstrating before the whole class, use at least one word or phrase in a language other than English.

Accommodations for Atypical Learners. Reconstructing sentences and phrases may be confusing for the child who is developing more slowly than most. Concentrate on the child's name first. Then move on to two-word phrases. Working one-on-one with a child offers a good opportunity to notice and follow up on problems that may be vision-related.

Accommodations for Advanced Learners. Stress reconstruction of dictation with children who are on the brink of writing on their own. Point out the spaces between the words. Have children choose a word from a sentence or phrase and spell it while pointing to the letters. Encourage them to try out writing on their own. Notice how they are gaining control over written language and demonstrating what they know. Have the child who is ready to attend to multiple words work with their messages cut into individual words. Figure 5.17 shows a child's dictated version of a picture story produced after hearing the book *Elephant, Hippopotamus, and Rabbit: The Tug of War* (Ncube, 2012). After watching the teacher label the parts of her drawing and write her dictated message, the print beneath Kristen's picture was copied onto a sentence strip that was then cut into individual words. Using the dictated message as a guide, Kristen was able to put the individual words in order and again read aloud the message with her teacher's assistance.

MAKING CONNECTIONS BETWEEN HOME AND SCHOOL

Use the information in Figure 5.18 to create your own flier to be sent home to parents or for use at a parents' meeting. This flier offers suggestions that parents can follow to assist their children in learning to write letters and words. Prepare the flier in more than one language, if necessary.

FIGURE 5.17. Drawing and dictated story reconstruction.

In school we are learning to write letters and words. We are discovering that . . .
- Lines of print contain individual letters.
- Letters are made with straight and curved lines.
- Words contain letters.
- We can listen to the sounds in words to decide what letters to write.

Learning to write letters and words is important because . . .
- Knowing how to write letters and words gives children an advantage in learning to read.
- Writing letters and creating words gives children another way to express their ideas.

Here are a few ways you can help:
- Provide your child with paper and crayons or washable markers so they can experiment with writing at home.
- Let your child help you write his or her name on their possessions when a label is needed.
- Let your child see you writing.
- Let your child help you write items on your grocery list or entries on your calendar.

FIGURE 5.18. Information for parents: Learning to write letters and words.

Myths about Alphabetic Knowledge for Writing

Writing instruction for preschool children should focus on uppercase letters only.

Children encounter both uppercase and lowercase letters as they interact with print in their environment, and they are curious about each. While systematic instruction of alphabet letters typically does begin with uppercase letters, teachers should model both uppercase and lowercase letters in their own writing and as they engage children in shared writing. Children will gain further exposure to both kinds of letters through environmental print and books. It is not uncommon for preschoolers to try both kinds of letters in their own writing. We shouldn't worry in the preschool years about where children use lowercase and uppercase letters. The concept of when to use each kind of letter, except perhaps in their own names, is too abstract for most preschool children. Knowing that there are two kinds of letters, big ones and little ones, and having a familiarity with how each looks, is plenty for children to know in these early years.

Every time teachers engage children in shared writing, their focus should be on print concepts.

Shared reading is an excellent vehicle for teaching children about print, as we have demonstrated in this chapter. Keep in mind, though, that not all interactions with print through shared reading and writing serve the same purpose. As we illustrated in Chapter 3, shared writing can also be used to support children's developing ability to compose meaningful texts or to help them record their thoughts about a book they have heard or an experience they have shared. In those instances, the primary focus is on authoring and shared meaning. When that is the purpose of instruction, frequently slowing down free-flowing sharing of ideas to overtly demonstrate print concepts will actually distract from the intended focus on meaning. In that case, it is sufficient to simply say the words aloud while children observe the writing. Be sure to use shared reading and writing activities for a variety of purposes and match the specific concepts demonstrated to the intended focus of the lesson.

IDEAS FOR DISCUSSION, REFLECTION, AND ACTION

1. Discuss the strategies offered in this chapter. How are they similar to things you are already doing? How are they different? What changes might you make to your curriculum to engage children more deeply in learning alphabetic knowledge for writing?

2. Observe a shared writing lesson with preschool children, either in another teacher's classroom or via a video found online. Discuss what you observe, keeping in mind the concepts preschool children need to learn as presented in this chapter. What specific knowledge are children likely to gain from the lesson you observe? How might the lesson be adapted to teach other concepts?

3. Examine one unit of your preschool curriculum. Based on the topics included and the books that will be shared with children, plan for two whole-class curriculum-related shared writing charts for each week of the unit. Also plan for additional shared writing demonstrations for other days that can be based on children's interests or perhaps related to morning message routines.

CHAPTER 6

Assessing Print Knowledge for Reading in Preschool

The children in Mrs. Delpit's preschool classroom had just finished creating a shared writing chart that summarized their visit to a local aquarium. It was now time for them to take turns stepping up to the chart to examine the print. That week, children were learning the letters *S*, *M*, and *T*. Mrs. Delpit asked Maci to find and circle the letter *T* anywhere on the chart. Maci didn't hesitate and immediately circled the *T* in the word *octopus*. Before Mrs. Delpit could call the next child to step up, Maci scanned the chart quickly and circled another *T* in the word *the*.

Eric stepped up next, and Mrs. Delpit asked him to find and circle the letter *S*. He looked over the five lines of print on the chart, but was not able to find an *S*. Mrs. Delpit pointed to the second line of print and said, "Can you find an *S* on this line?" Once again, Eric was unable to do so. Mrs. Delpit then held up a magnetic letter *S* and said, "This is an *S*. Can you find a letter in this line that looks like this?" Eric then ran his finger under each word, continuously looking at the letter she held until he was able to locate an *S* in the word *seahorse*. He pointed to the letter and looked questioningly at Mrs. Delpit. "That's right!" she said. "That is an *S*. Can you circle it for me?"

To even a casual observer of this lesson, it would be apparent that Maci and Eric differed in their knowledge of early literacy. Maci was very confident in her knowledge of the letter she was asked to find. Eric, on the other hand, clearly had not yet solidified his knowledge of the letter *S*. When Mrs. Delpit made the task somewhat easier by directing him to look for an *S* in a single line of print, Eric was still unable to do so. It was only when Mrs. Delpit showed him what the letter looked like that he was able to find a matching symbol. Even as he circled the letter after significant scaffolding from Mrs. Delpit, it was clear that he had not actually learned to associate the print letter with the correct letter name.

It is likely that Maci and Eric are at very different levels in their early literacy development and may require differentiated support as they continue to learn about print. Wide differences like these in children's skills and abilities within the same classroom are common throughout all grades, but nowhere more so than in preschool. Despite significant variation in development among preschool children, their teachers are increasingly accountable for moving all children toward benchmarks that indicate readiness for kindergarten. This accountability often translates into requirements to assess even the youngest children's learning. In the United States, federal mandates have focused a spotlight on early literacy learning in particular, heightening discussion about the importance of ensuring that all children arrive at kindergarten ready to benefit from the more intensive instruction that characterizes the start of formal schooling (Casbergue, 2010).

A dilemma for preschool teachers is how to determine if children are making adequate progress toward kindergarten readiness and how to judge which children will need more intensive instruction, particularly in the area of early literacy upon which many measures of readiness are based. Early screening using standardized assessments combined with continuous observational documentation of children's literacy learning will offer teachers the information they need to design appropriate individualized instruction and demonstrate children's levels of readiness.

STANDARDIZED ASSESSMENTS OF PRINT KNOWLEDGE

Teachers need to assess where children are in their literacy development when they first enter a preschool classroom. Doing so helps them begin to identify children who might need more intensive support as well as those who might need enrichment beyond the general curriculum. Even with groups of students drawn from the same community and sharing similar socioeconomic status and family characteristics, it is almost always the case that some children will arrive for the first day of preschool already knowing many alphabet letters, familiar with concepts about print, and perhaps even writing their names, while others will not recognize any letters, have little familiarity with print concepts, and write even their own names with scribbles.

With effective instruction that takes into account these significant differences, however, it is possible for most children to reach levels of early literacy that suggest they are ready for kindergarten. Figure 6.1 includes the actual results of one readiness screening assessment given at the start of the preschool year (the diamond data points) and again at the end of the year (the square data points) in a preschool classroom participating in an Early Reading First (ERF) project. Each

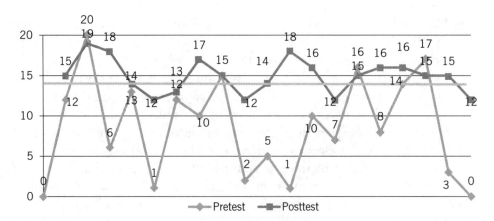

FIGURE 6.1. GRTR assessment results.

diamond-shaped data point represents a single child's score on the Get Ready to Read (GRTR) screening test (Whitehurst & Lonigan, 2001). The straight line at point 14 indicates the benchmark for kindergarten readiness.

The differences in children's knowledge of print upon school entry are startling, although not at all unfamiliar to teachers who work with children in high-poverty communities like those served by ERF federally funded programs. You can see that six of the children were able to respond correctly to three or fewer items on the test at the beginning of the year. (Note that these results are from the original 20-item edition of the GRTR.) Equally important, five other children scored at or above the kindergarten readiness benchmark upon preschool entry. Obviously, this is very important information for teachers to have as they begin to prepare for teaching all of these children!

Get Ready to Read—Revised (GRTR-R; Whitehurst & Lonigan, 2010) is a brief screening instrument that is simple to administer. It is individually administered and takes about 10 minutes for each child assessed. The online version is free and can be found at *www.getreadytoread.org/screening-tools/grtr-screening-tool/the-tool*. An inexpensive print version of the assessment is also available. The revised edition contains 25 items that assess print knowledge (a child's understanding of books, printed letters, and words), linguistic awareness (a child's understanding of how words and language work), and emergent writing (a child's first efforts to create and use print in a meaningful way). For all but the writing assessment, children view a series of four pictures while the teacher reads aloud instructions, and then simply point to the picture representing their response. Because of the brevity of this screening instrument, it does not provide a comprehensive view of what children do or don't know about print. Rather, it offers a standardized assessment that indicates where children are in their emergent literacy knowledge and skill relative to each other and to the population of children on which the test was normed to establish the benchmark for kindergarten readiness.

Another formal assessment that does offer more specific information about children's emergent literacy is the Test of Preschool Early Literacy (TOPEL; Lonigan, Wagner, & Torgesen, 2007). It contains three subtests that address print knowledge, definitional vocabulary, and phonological awareness.

The print awareness subtest consists of 36 items designed to measure early knowledge about written language conventions and form, as well as alphabet knowledge. Children are asked to point to aspects of print, identify letters and written words, point to specific letters, name specific letters, say the sounds associated with specific letters, and identify letters associated with specific sounds.

The definitional vocabulary subtest contains 35 items that measure a child's single-word oral vocabulary and definitional vocabulary. For each picture children are shown, they are first asked to tell what it is, and then asked to respond to a question about one of its important features or attributes. For example, they may identify a picture of a turtle, and then answer a question that asks if it is fast or slow. In this way, the subtest assesses both surface vocabulary knowledge and deep vocabulary knowledge.

The phonological awareness subtest has 27 items that measure a child's ability to manipulate the sounds of language. Part of the subtest requires the child to say a word, then to say what is left after dropping out specific sounds. For example, a prompt might be, "Say *heat* without the /t/ sound." The remaining items require listening to separate sounds and combining them to form a word. For example, a child might be asked to combine the sounds /ca/ and /p/ to form the word *cap*—a traditional blending task.

Standardized scores are derived from the individual subtests and then combined into a composite score for overall performance. The results of this test can serve two purposes for preschool teachers: to identify children who are likely to have problems learning to read and write, and to document progress in early literacy-related skills as a result of regular classroom instruction or more targeted intervention. The TOPEL is individually administered, and takes about 30 minutes for each child.

Assessments like GRTR and TOPEL, as well as others such as Phonological Awareness Literacy Screening (PALS-PreK; Invernizzi, Sullivan, Meier, & Swank, 2004) are best used at the beginning of the school year to identify children's relative strengths and weaknesses, and at the middle and end of the school year to measure progress after instruction. These assessments are research-based; the types of skills they assess have been demonstrated to relate to children's later success with literacy learning (NELP, 2008; Snow et al., 1998).

A concern with these tests, however, is that they do not assess children's use of print knowledge and concepts about print in the context of actual reading and handling of books. They may choose the picture that shows the back of a book, for example, but do not actually handle a real book to demonstrate that they know the front from the back. One classic assessment designed to overcome this shortcoming is Marie Clay's Concepts about Print Test, which is included in *The Early*

Detection of Reading Difficulties: A Diagnostic Survey with Recovery Procedures (Clay, 1979). This assessment offers two 20-page paperback books, *Sand* and *Stones*, that are designed to resemble typical children's trade books. As children handle these books, they are prompted to respond in ways that reveal an array of knowledge about book handling and print concepts. One set of items addresses concepts about book orientation. These items provide insight into whether children know how to orient a book to begin reading from the front and whether they recognize when a book, pictures, or print are right-side up or upside-down. Another set of items addresses concepts about whether print or pictures carry the message of the text. These items ask the child to point to where the test administrator is reading as the book is read aloud to the child. Additional items address concepts about directionality of lines of print, sequence of pages, and directionality of words. For these items, the child is asked to follow along with a finger and point as the teacher is reading. In addition, children are asked to say what is wrong on pages that have lines of print, letters, or words out of order. Concepts about the relationship between written and oral language are also assessed with observation and documentation of how well the child can track print on particular pages while pointing as the observer reads. Finally, concepts of words, letters, capitals, space, and punctuation are addressed as children are asked to talk about print conventions and point to these items.

While the test does offer norms for children at age 6, certainly outside the preschool age range, that is primarily because the assessment was designed to identify children who should be placed in Reading Recovery, a first-grade intervention. Nonetheless, the items are very relevant to the kinds of print knowledge now commonly assessed as children are screened for kindergarten readiness. This is especially true now that attention to early literacy in preschool has accelerated. Indeed, in her review of this assessment, Goodman (1981) suggested that the test is best used to gain insights into the knowledge of individual children: "It need not be used to obtain norm-referenced scores but may be used very profitably for developmental insights into the individual" (p. 447). This assessment, with standardized administration procedures, requires about 15 minutes per child.

All of the formal assessments described thus far are not intended for regular ongoing assessment of children's learning about print. Few preschool teachers would be able to find the time to do weekly or even monthly individual testing of each child in their classrooms, particularly using the more detailed (but also more informative) assessments like the TOPEL and Concepts about Print Test. Yet they do need to know how children are responding to instruction at regular intervals. Teachers often overestimate preschoolers' knowledge based on how the children respond to instruction when they are part of a whole-class lesson or even when they are engaged in small-group instruction. Participating in literacy learning activities with a group of other children itself provides scaffolding that some children depend on to respond to teachers' questions and prompts. It is likely that

Eric, who struggled to find a letter *S* in the vignette that opened this chapter, would have been able to respond correctly with his peers when asked to identify the letter during group instruction. When a teacher holds up a letter card for children to identify, the whole group is likely to blurt out the correct response. Careful observation will reveal, however, that some children hesitate for a second, chiming in when they hear how other children respond. Some teachers take those group responses as affirmation that the children have, indeed, learned what is being taught. Since that is not always the case, it is important for teachers to determine what individual children do and do not know after instruction. This kind of classroom-based ongoing assessment that directly measures knowledge and skills being taught is crucial to planning effective instruction.

CLASSROOM-BASED ASSESSMENT OF EARLY LITERACY LEARNING

Classroom-based assessment, that is, teacher-constructed measures of children's learning of specific concepts addressed in instruction, offers an avenue for tracking children's early literacy learning as frequently as new concepts are taught. It is typical for early literacy curricula to introduce new letters, letter sounds, and vocabulary each week, for example. After a series of lessons devoted to teaching those letters, sounds, and words, teachers can—and should— determine what children have actually learned.

Through curriculum-based assessment, assessment directly tied to specific concepts being taught, preschool teachers may find, for example, that most of the children can consistently identify two of the three letters taught in a particular week, but only a few know the third. They may find that most children can give names for all five of the vocabulary words explicitly taught that week, but only demonstrate definitional knowledge of two of them. Findings like these let teachers know which items need to be taught again or continually emphasized the following week—even as new letters and words are introduced. They may also discover that some individual children struggle with even those concepts apparently mastered by most of the class. That information can be used to design specialized intervention for a small group of children who need more time and focused instruction to achieve the same level of understanding that their classmates were able to demonstrate in response to the general curriculum activities.

Teacher-Constructed Systematic Assessment

Teachers can design their own curriculum-based assessments using the same materials they use for instruction. Systematically assessing children's knowledge each week can be as simple as asking children to identify that week's target letters and sounds (and perhaps those from previous lessons as well) and give definitional vocabulary for target vocabulary words in response to pictures. A checklist like that in Figure 6.2 can be completed for each child and placed in his or her assessment folder to be used for planning individualized and small group instruction.

Teachers can use a template of this form to fill in the specific letters and vocabulary words that are the focus of instruction each week, then test children quickly by calling them over one at a time during their free play in centers or while a teaching assistant leads whole-class activities. With materials prepared ahead of time, it is possible to assess up to 20 children in a single day at the end of the week. Similar checklists can be constructed to assess children's knowledge of other print concepts or ability to blend and segment sounds, depending of course on the content of the early literacy curriculum for a given week.

As an alternative to tests they design themselves, teachers can create assessments within the Curriculum-Based Decision Making Assessment system (CBDM; Burstein & Ergul, 2009; Roskos et al, 2008). CBDM is an online tool for building, administering, and interpreting short, reliable tests of specific literacy concepts appropriate for use in preschool through second grade. Information about the system can be found at *http://CBDM.defaultroute.net/CBDM.education*. Its literacy component includes a system of six item banks that contain over 6,000 words, numbers, questions, and readings. There are 12 test templates (two for letter naming, three for vocabulary, two for phonological awareness, one for phonics, three for comprehension, and one for print awareness) that classroom teachers can use to select and organize items that assess early literacy skills taught in their classrooms. CBDM users typically identify key skills recently taught, and then identify items that reflect those skills to create and administer tests.

The test construction process takes approximately 10 minutes and administration typically takes 3–5 minutes per test. Teachers can create tests with as few or as many items as they wish. When used in multiple ERF projects across the United States, most preschool teachers created tests that assessed four to six letter names, four to six letter sounds, and four to six expressive and receptive vocabulary words each week. CBDM output provides immediate feedback on what children have learned and areas of difficulty. Outcomes include individual and group comparisons across time and trend lines of children's progress.

In most of the ERF projects using the CBDM, teachers were given the option to test a representative sample of children each week to assess their response to instruction. They were encouraged to select two children from among the lowest performing group identified on initial screening tests, two children whose performance was average among their peers, and two children whose achievement was above average. While some teachers did use this approach, most found the information valuable enough that they decided on their own to test all of the children in the classroom on a weekly basis. In many cases, this use of the assessment enabled them to comply with school or school-system mandates to demonstrate their use of data-driven instruction.

Name: _____   Date: _____

Letters tested	Letter names		Letter sounds		Comments
	Yes	No	Yes	No	
S					
T					
O					
M					
C					
A					

Vocabulary words	Word name		Definitional		Comments
	Yes	No	Yes	No	
lightning					
kennel					
antenna					
shivering					

FIGURE 6.2. Weekly formative assessment checklist.

Ongoing Observational Assessment

While a system of weekly curriculum-based assessments is a valuable component of preschool early literacy programs, teachers can glean significant additional insight about children's emerging knowledge of literacy concepts by observing as they interact with print throughout the day. It was this idea that led Marie Clay to create one of the first observational assessments of children's emerging literacy skills, including her Concepts about Print Test described earlier (Clay, 1979). While the *Sands* and *Stones* books cannot be used repeatedly for ongoing assessment, many of the items included in her test can be used with any books children are reading. Teachers can ask preschoolers to point out features of print and observe how they handle books very quickly when children go to the library center during center activities.

As we have demonstrated in the previous chapters, though, preschool children engage with print for multiple purposes throughout the day—not just in the library or writing centers. Whether in self-directed activities such as dramatic play or in teacher-directed activities like shared reading and shared writing, a classroom that is print-rich offers children many opportunities to engage with books and other print. Use of surveys like Clay's or other checklists of essential skills will facilitate documentation of children's emerging literacy.

Most teachers are adept at noticing when children demonstrate new learning. Not all take the time to document those observations, however, perhaps believing they will remember those demonstrations of knowledge when necessary. Given the number of children teachers work with every day, though, it is likely that much information is lost. Teachers who have become proficient in observational assessment develop the habit of taking anecdotal notes about any significant behaviors they observe. Keeping a small notepad handy to jot down brief notes about what is observed will facilitate this process. Those initial notes can be fleshed out at the end of the day with more contextual information and instructional implications and then placed in children's assessment folders. An initial anecdotal note about Eric's interaction with print during shared writing, for example, might say:

> "Shared writing—circling letters. Could not locate *S* on full chart. Directed to one line. Needed to see model of letter."

At the end of the day, the teacher might add her observation about Eric's need to look back at the letter frequently as he scanned each word in the line of print, and his hesitancy once he found the correct letter. She might also indicate her instructional plan for intervention with Eric, noting perhaps her intention to offer him more opportunities for tactile / kinesthetic exploration of target letters.

As anecdotal notes are collected over time, teachers will begin to compile a fuller picture of children's early literacy than they can derive from tests alone. In addition to revealing what children do and don't know, these notes will illuminate in which contexts and under which conditions children are able to demonstrate knowledge of print concepts. If instructional intentions are included, they can also serve to document both strategies that were implemented and children's responses to instruction.

KNOWING WHAT TO LOOK FOR

A key to taking useful anecdotal notes is knowing what to look for! There are many ways that children show us that they are learning. Depending on the activity in which children are engaged, teachers can watch for variety of literate behaviors. These range from book-handling skills to knowledge of the alphabet and understanding of the alphabetic principle.

Knowledge about Books

Preschool children demonstrate understanding of books whenever they handle them. Look to see how the youngest children hold a book. Do they orient it correctly from top to bottom? Do they begin turning pages from the front to the back of the book? For older preschool children, notice if they attend to the title of books as they select them. Can they locate specific favorite books or books with information they seek using the titles and pictures on the cover? When prompted by the teacher during read-aloud, can they point to the author's and illustrator's names on a book cover? Are they aware of what authors and illustrators do? These very basic skills represent children's growing understanding of the purpose of books and how to use them.

Knowledge about Environmental Print

Document when you observe children using environmental print in the classroom. Do they notice and use labels on storage containers when they clean up after play-time? Do they show interest in posters of poems, nursery rhymes, or songs displayed on classroom walls? Do they notice and use print artifacts in their dramatic play? Do they find and copy words from environmental print in their own writing? Documenting when and how frequently children engage with environmental print will reveal which children are developing significant interest in print and which children might need extra encouragement to do so. Attending to children's use of environmental print also lets us know that they understand that print carries meaning and signals what people say when they read—a basic understanding critical to learning finer aspects of textural features and the alphabetic principle.

Knowledge of the Concepts of Letters and Words

Make note when children first begin to indicate that they understand what a word is and that words are comprised of letters. Listen as they talk about print. Do they indicate that print or even scribbles on their paper are "words?" Even if marks aren't recognizable as words, when children use that term to refer to what they have written we know that they are beginning to develop the concept of word. The same is true when children refer to "letters." Growing awareness of the concept of word and the concept of letter is also evident when children ask adults how to write words or letters, or when they refer to words or letters when talking to other children about what they are doing. An anecdotal note when teachers notice a child first developing these concepts will document this important conceptual development.

Phonological and Phonemic Awareness

Observe as children participate in reciting nursery rhymes or favorite poems. They will show signs of developing phonological awareness when they can play with rhymes and chime in with rhyming words when the teacher pauses while reading aloud. Also notice when they are able to hear distinct syllables in words. As children participate in games like clapping their names (as described in Chapter 4), look for their ability to hear the parts in their own and in their classmates' names.

Finer-grained phonemic awareness will be evident as children participate in games or sing songs that invite them to manipulate sounds in words. Many of us have had fun leading children in singing "The Name Game"—"David David bo bavid, banana fanna fo favid, fe fi mo mavid, David!"—or the Raffi "Apples and Bananas" song—"I like to eat, eat, eat, eeples and beneenies, I like to oat, oat, oat, oples and bononos." Notice which children can take the lead singing the songs, and which ones respond more slowly. Finally, observe children as they work independently with sorting objects or picture cards according to initial or ending sounds in the writing center or table games area. Make note of which children are able to sort correctly, as well as which sounds they hear most readily and the ones with which they struggle.

Knowledge of the Alphabet

Preschool children's ability to recognize and name alphabet letters is measured very easily through quick tests using either commercially prepared instruments or teacher-made checklists described earlier in this chapter. Teachers can also observe children's knowledge of the alphabet through observation as they engage with environmental print, work with materials in the writing center, and read alphabet books. Figure 6.3 is an example of an opportunity to document one child's alphabet knowledge through a regular classroom routine. Notice and document when children demonstrate awareness of both uppercase and lowercase letters. Try to document when children first begin to exhibit interest in and curiosity about alphabet letters.

Knowledge of the Alphabetic Principle

Preschoolers' ability to match the sounds of words to corresponding letters of the alphabet can be observed as children participate in many activities. When they engage in picture- or object-sorting activities based on specific letter sounds, we can assess and document the extent to which they can apply letter–sound knowledge. Shared reading and writing lessons offer particularly potent opportunities to observe children's growing knowledge of the alphabetic principal, especially as children are invited to step up to engage with the print on shared reading and writing charts as described in Chapters 4 and 5. If they are invited to find and circle a specific letter, they are demonstrating knowledge of the alphabet. If instead, they are invited to find and circle a word that begins with a particular *sound*, they then demonstrate the alphabetic principle. In addition to observing and making notes about children's responses during shared reading and writing lessons, make note of children's interactions with those materials when they are made available for children's independent inspection during center activities.

Knowledge of Words

While we do not expect that most preschool children will be able to read words conventionally, even as they are ready to enter kindergarten, some children do, in

FIGURE 6.3. Observing a child's participation for assessment.

fact, begin to display this ability. When they do so, it is worth documenting—and celebrating! Notice when children first become aware of and comment on contextualized environmental print. Many classrooms have two doors into the hallway. Some use one to enter and another to exit the classroom, labeling the doors with "In" and "Out" signs. In this case, when the teacher has called children's attention to these words as they pass through the doorways, some children will begin to recognize those words. Many children will recognize the word "STOP" when it is written on a red background. Notice when children demonstrate that they can read common words like these, even in different contexts—perhaps on signs in the block center or on props in dramatic play. Also notice which children are able to locate words in the classroom while playing "word hunt" games like those described in Chapter 4. Do they have to match letter by letter, or are they able to find and read the matching word as a whole? Observing as children interact with print across many activities and in a variety of different classroom contexts will provide a full picture of children's knowledge of words.

CHECKLISTS OF EARLY PRINT KNOWLEDGE

What should we look for as evidence of children's emerging literacy development? Obviously, there is quite a lot to look for. Teachers may consider using checklists periodically to do a quick assessment of the literacy behaviors children display. Alternately, checklists can be placed inside the notepad used for anecdotal notes as an abbreviated reminder of what to notice and document. Figure 6.4 is a checklist that summarizes knowledge of concepts of print. Figure 6.5 is a checklist to be used for assessing print awareness and book handling.

Use of checklists offers a way to conduct quick assessments of children at frequent intervals. Their use enables teachers to collect assessment data for all children, even those who do not frequently engage with print outside of teacher-led instructional activities. Teachers may want to establish an assessment schedule whereby they systematically collect assessment information on a different small group of focal children each week. They can begin with careful observation of those specific children to see how and when they choose to use print, and then invite children to participate in brief individual assessment activities guided by checklists.

INSTRUCTIONAL IMPLICATIONS OF READING ASSESSMENT

As is the case with all assessments, assessment information about children's emerging reading ability is pointless unless it is used to inform instruction. While screening assessment at the start of a school year may give teachers initial ideas about which children are advanced and in need of extra enrichment and which ones may need intensive intervention, children's literacy knowledge is never static. Some children who start out behind their peers may gain knowledge and skills very rapidly in response to high-quality instruction. And some children who start out doing well may struggle and progress more slowly than their peers. As children change over time, so too must the instruction they receive. Teachers need to decide, sometimes on a weekly basis, which children need special intervention lessons and which children require more challenging activities to enhance their

---

Observe children's understanding of the following concepts:

Print Conveys Meaning

_____ Writing is a way to express ideas.

Directionality

Speech is written from _____ left to right and _____ top to bottom.

Concept of Word

_____ Words are composed of letters.

_____ Words match to speech.

_____ There are spaces between words.

Letter Knowledge

_____ Correct letter names are used.

Phonemic Awareness

_____ Some words have the same beginning sounds. (The child is beginning to perceive some relationship between the sounds and letters.)

Literacy Language

_____ Certain words (e.g., *word, letter, story, author*) are used to talk about reading and writing.

FIGURE 6.4. Observation checklist for assessing children's knowledge of concepts of print.

literacy development. Those decisions must be based on the most current evidence possible of children's learning and development.

A combination of both initial screening assessments and ongoing curriculum-based assessment will ensure that teachers are equipped to make crucial decisions about what and how to teach early literacy. Instruction that is responsive to children's developmental abilities and their individual needs as determined through assessment will result in children who are ready take off as readers!

Instructions: Administer to one child at a time with a familiar book. You may also observe for these concepts during group activities.

Book Handling

1. ____ What would you need if you wanted me to read a story to you?
2. ____ (Show a book.) What do you do with this?
3. ____ Show me the front of the book.
4. ____ Show me a page in the book.
5. ____ Where should I start reading it?
6. ____ (Show the beginning of a line.) If I start here, which way do I go when I read?
7. ____ Where is the top of the page?
8. ____ Where is the bottom of the page?

Print Awareness

9. ____ Can you show me a word on the page?
10. ____ Can you show me a letter?
    a. ____ Upper-case (capital)?
    b. ____ Lower-case (small)?
11. ____ (Show a scribble.) Is this a word?
12. ____ (Show a well-known logo such as McDonald's or Coca Cola.)
    a. ____ What does this tell about?
    b. ____ Where does it say _____?
    c. ____ Are you reading that?
    d. ____ (Print the word.) What does this say?

FIGURE 6.5. Print awareness and book-handling assessment checklist.

A Myth about Preschool Literacy Assessment

The screening assessment I am required to do before the start of the school year tells me which children will need intervention for everything I teach this year. I need to be sure to always plan different lessons for those children.

While it is true that screening assessments suggest which children we need to attend to more closely, even the most valid and reliable measures give us at best a single snapshot of a child's capabilities. We have already described how rapidly children's learning and development may advance once they begin to receive effective early literacy instruction. Teachers need to be very careful not to label children, whether as struggling, as normally achieving, or as advanced, based on initial assessments. Especially upon preschool entry, children's demonstrated abilities are very much related to the experiences they have had in early childhood. It is the case that some very bright, capable children simply have not had significant opportunity to interact with print before coming to preschool. Once they are in a print-rich environment, they may rapidly gain concepts about print in response to normal instructional activities.

It is equally problematic to assume that children who test poorly or exceptionally well on screening tests will display similar performance in all areas of the curriculum. Some children may arrive at preschool already recognizing most of the letters of the alphabet, well above expectations, yet have significant difficulty learning letter sounds. Children that arrive knowing many concepts about print, suggesting lots of prior experience with books, may nonetheless struggle to learn the alphabet. That is why it is so important for teachers to assess multiple areas of literacy and to do so frequently in order to design effective instruction.

IDEAS FOR DISCUSSION, REFLECTION, AND ACTION

1. Ask yourself, "How much do I notice what individual children are doing when they interact with print?" Reflect on a typical day in your classroom. Are there particular centers in which children are most likely to examine print as part of their play? How much time do you spend in those centers so you can observe and document children's growing knowledge of print?

2. Do the children in your classroom notice and use shared writing charts and large print materials from shared reading after teacher-directed lessons have concluded? Reflect on how you might extend whole-class instructional activities into center activities, giving children more opportunities to interact with print and giving yourself additional opportunities to observe and document their learning.

3. With other preschool teachers who share your curriculum, examine each unit for the print-related skills that are to be taught. Use the templates in Figure 6.2 to develop quick assessments for each week of instruction.

4. Use the checklists in Figures 6.3 and 6.4 to observe two children as they participate in whole-class and small-group instruction as well as during center activities. Note which contexts offer the best opportunities to document different kinds of literacy behavior. Also notice how similar and different the two children are in when and how they engage with print.

CHAPTER 7

Assessing Writing Development in Preschool

Four-year-old Emilio worked diligently in the writing center, using one crayon after another to shade in different portions of his paper. When he had filled the page with colors, he wrote an *M* at the bottom. Next to the *M*, he then carefully copied the word "Crayons" from a Crayola box.

When his teacher, Mrs. Jenkins, joined him in the writing center, he showed her his page, saying, "I put lots of colors."

Mrs. Jenkins said, "And I see that you wrote, 'My crayons' at the bottom. Did you copy the word 'crayons' from somewhere?"

Emilio looked puzzled for a moment as he examined the letters at the bottom of the page. "That says, 'My colors!'" he responded.

As we discussed in Chapter 6, preschool teachers must assess children's progress in multiple areas of development. Children's writing development is no exception. As with assessment of print knowledge for reading, teachers may turn to commercially prepared or teacher-made assessments when they need to measure children's knowledge about writing. There are very few formal early literacy assessments, however, that include measures of emergent writing for children as early as preschool. As mentioned in Chapter 6, the GRTR-R (Whitehurst & Lonigan, 2010) includes a brief five-item subtest related to writing. The Test of Early Written Language (TEWL-3; Hresko, Herron, Peak, & Hicks, 2012) is another standardized assessment that offers more extensive measures of knowledge about print and writing. It has two subtests, Basic Writing, and Contextual Writing, although only the Basic Writing subtest provides norms for 4-year-old children.

Norms for Contextual Writing, a subtest in which children write in response to a picture prompt, begin at age 5. That subtest would only be appropriate, therefore, for the very oldest preschool children. The Basic Writing subtest can be used with 4-year-olds; it consists of 70 items of increasing difficulty (covering ages 4–11) designed to measure a child's understanding about language and his or her ability to use the writing tools of language. Only a portion of those items would be used with typical 4-year-olds. For these youngest children, this subtest offers an indication of their metalinguistic knowledge, understanding of directionality, and awareness of letter features.

Formal assessments like the TEWL-3 are sometimes used before and after intervention programs to determine specific effects of instruction. They can also be used to screen children upon program entry to determine if they are significantly above or below their classmates' level of achievement and thus in need of special accommodations. Most often, though, they are used in clinical settings to identify children at risk for learning difficulties and in need of specialized services outside of the regular preschool program.

A benefit of the assessment information derived from standardized assessments is that they provide norms against which individual children's performance can be measured. This enables a teacher to determine which children may require more intensive instruction in order to achieve on par with typical children their age. Standardized tests have been criticized, however, for requiring very young children to engage in tasks that are completely unfamiliar to them. For writing in particular, standardized assessments ask children to complete decontextualized tasks that are far removed from what they actually do when they define their own purposes for writing. These tests are also criticized for their focus on discrete skills like the ability to write individual alphabet letters properly, again outside of a meaningful purpose for which a preschool child might write. For these reasons, standardized writing assessment is not recommended as the best means of documenting children's writing ability or progress in a preschool setting.

Nonetheless, while preschool teachers are only rarely required to administer formal standardized assessments, they are expected to be aware of each child's progress and to design teacher-directed instruction as well as play opportunities that accommodate children's varying levels of skill. At the preschool level, this can be done by carefully observing and documenting children's demonstrations of progress. Teachers can document changes by taking note of the varied ways that children attempt to write and by preserving samples of children's drawing and writing over a period of time. As Emilio's reading of his own writing suggests, however, simply examining children's written products is not sufficient for accurately addressing what children know, and do not know, about writing. Comprehensive writing assessment also requires careful attention to the contexts within which children write. We must be aware of children's intentions and the process they use while writing to develop a full picture of writing development.

If Mrs. Jenkins had simply examined Emilio's writing without speaking to him about what he had written, she might have made the following assumption:

- Emilio's message creation includes writing simple labels for his drawing.
- Emilio shows some evidence of applying the alphabetic principle in his word creation efforts (e.g., using the letter *M* to write the word *my*).
- Emilio uses conventional alphabet letters when he writes *(MCRAYONS)*.
- Emilio knows how to seek out environmental print for words he wants to write.
- Emilio can read and copy contextualized environmental print accurately (e.g., copying from the Crayola box to write the word *crayons*).

While her conclusions about his message creation, phonemic spelling, and mark making would have been correct, assumptions about Emilio's use of environmental print and word creation would not have been entirely accurate. He could not actually read the word *crayons* on the box. Instead, he did a highly contextualized reading to decide that the label on the box said "colors," perhaps aided by the hard /c/ sound at the beginning of both words. Emilio's writing process emphasizes the importance of documenting as much as possible about how children's writing is created. Examining children's written products without observing how they were produced can lead a teacher to conclude that children know more than they actually do.

Teachers also need to remember that the kinds of writing children do will vary depending on context. A child might use early phonemic spelling when writing a story at the writing center, for example, but use lines of letter strings or scribble to create a pretend grocery list in dramatic play when the writing is clearly make-believe. If samples from dramatic play are the only ones considered, teachers might underestimate children's level of skill.

CAPTURING MULTIPLE DIMENSIONS OF WRITING

Thus, it should be evident that children's writing development is multidimensional. That is, children must learn how to make marks, moving from scribbles to recognizable alphabet letters. They must also learn to create words, starting with strings of symbols (i.e., mock letters) without any consideration of representing sounds, and moving gradually to the use of alphabet letters that are selected to represent sounds in spoken words. At the same time, they also learn how to create messages that range from simple labels to full stories and compositions that share information. Full assessment of children's writing development requires a teacher to examine all of these dimensions simultaneously because children might, for example, be fairly advanced in message creation, while using only rudimentary drawings with little use of print, sometimes at the scribble level.

Examination of children's written products along with observation of how those products are created enables teachers to accurately assess these multiple dimensions of writing. Consider the picture in Figure 7.1. The child on the left, Grayson, wanted to write an invitation for a pretend party. Her teacher explained that an invitation should include the time and place of the event, as well as the hostesses' names. Because the teacher was a participant in this writing event, she was aware that Grayson did not create this message by herself. Instead, she was told what this particular cultural artifact should say. Given the circumstances, the teacher would not be able to judge, on the basis of this writing sample alone, the child's true message-creation skill. But the teacher watched as the child wrote, "6:30 Com To the PRPt FROm Lara Beth Grayson" by herself. Her marks, all conventional numbers and letters, and words—both invented and conventionally spelled—were produced independently and revealed very sophisticated skill on these dimensions of writing.

Notice that Laura, the child on the right in Figure 7.1, is also creating an invitation. She used her classmate's model, however, carefully copying the lines of print. It is not possible, therefore, to draw conclusions about the second child's independent level of skill beyond her ability to form alphabet letters, given her reliance on the support offered by both the teacher and Grayson. Had the teacher examined the two pieces of writing, without having observed their creation, she might have drawn some erroneous conclusions about the skills of each child.

As this example illustrates, simply gathering and preserving writing samples as the only means of documenting children's writing development is insufficient. All samples used for systematic assessment, or at least a majority, should be accompanied by anecdotal notes: brief descriptions of how and where the writing was

FIGURE 7.1. Writing an invitation in dramatic play.

produced, including who was present, what help they provided, the questions a child asked, what the child intended the writing to say, whether the child copied writing from some source, and so on. Only then can a teacher analyze the samples accurately to determine the child's understandings and skills. An anecdotal note to accompany the first child's invitation might read as follows:

> "Grayson initiated invitation writing during dramatic play. Teacher helped decide what to write. Wrote independently after discussion. First time she included vowels in invented spelling (com, from). Later helped Laura copy invitation."

To be useful, a good anecdotal note should provide enough context for the teacher to later remember the situation in which the writing occurred. A collection of such samples and anecdotal notes, gathered over time, serves multiple purposes. The samples capture and make visible children's writing development, provide tangible documentation to support a teacher's conclusions about children's skill levels, and provide evidence to share with parents, the child's future teachers, and administrators who might not otherwise understand the rich variety of ways in which children's writing develops.

THE CONTINUUM OF WRITING DEVELOPMENT

While it is fairly easy to describe the context within which specific writing samples are created, analyzing the samples is trickier, precisely because so many different skills develop simultaneously, and because specific contexts affect what and how children write. The continuum of writing development that follows, first described in Schickedanz and Casbergue (2008), provides an overview of each dimension (marks, word creation, and messages) and includes samples of writing to illustrate movement from simple to more advanced skills levels within each dimension. Preschool teachers can compare samples of writing and drawing collected from children in their own classrooms to the examples in the continuum to determine each child's developmental progress. Teachers can use this knowledge of children's writing development to tailor the instructional activities and manipulative materials they provide and to structure their interactions with children according to individual strengths and needs.

ASSESSING MARK MAKING

This part of the continuum concerns the physical characteristics of the marks children use when their intention is to write. Typically, when young children first intend to represent meanings, they draw rather than write. The continuum provided here, however, includes only levels of writing marks, not levels of picture making. You may wish to consult other resources to learn about levels of development for drawing and painting, such as Cherney, Seiwert, Dickey, and Flichtbeil (2006), Gardner (1980), or Picard and Gauthier (2012). Writing mark levels include (1) scribble, (2) mock letters, (3) actual letters (rudimentary approximations), (4) actual letters (closer approximations), and (5) actual letters (conventional). The most common levels seen in the preschool years are levels 1 through 3—which we discuss in the sections that follow—although some older preschoolers reach levels 4 and 5.

Children first use scribble marks for writing. Development within scribble writing moves from (1) marks organized very much like scribble drawings (i.e., no linear arrangement), to (2) continuous linear scribble without much internal detail, to (3) continuous linear scribble with internal detail, to (4) discrete scribble marks arranged in a line (see Figure 7.2). Determining whether a picture-like scribble is writing rather than drawing requires knowledge of the context and the child's intentions (e.g., child turns a collage paper over, scribbles on the back, and says, "I did my name").

When children notice the ways that lines are combined to make alphabet letters, they begin to create mock letters, that is, forms that look very much like the "real thing" (see Figure 7.3). Many preschoolers do not yet know that there are only 26 alphabet letters in the English alphabet, with a big and small form for each one. They might think there are countless letters that they have not yet seen and they create forms that are good possibilities! Often, preschoolers' mock letters are mixed in with actual letter forms because they seem to assume that the mock letters they create *could* be real letters, just ones they have not yet encountered in their environment.

Children's first actual letters are rudimentary—just a beginning. Their lines "wobble," overrun stopping points, are sometimes substitutions for a line in the conventional letter, are placed to create atypical proportions, and are often reversed (see Figure 7.4a). Over the preschool and kindergarten years, children's letters gradually develop into forms that resemble the conventional forms more closely (see Figure 7.4b) and then do match the conventional forms (see Figure 7.4c). Children's skill in forming specific letters is not "all or none" but varies across different letters. Some are harder to form than others, and a child's experience with different letters also affects skill in writing them. Preschoolers often can form best the first letter in their names, perhaps because they have focused on this letter the most when viewing their names, or because they have written only this letter for a period of time to stand for their entire name.

Even though a few preschool children write letters that are fully conventional, this is the exception not the rule. Forming letters conventionally requires fine motor skill beyond what is typical for most preschoolers, along with very detailed knowledge of letter features and how to combine lines to create these.

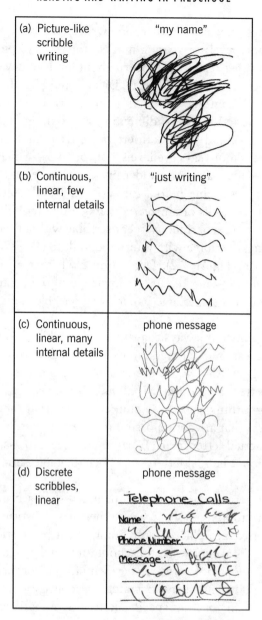

FIGURE 7.2. Examples of scribble writing.

FIGURE 7.3. Examples of mock letters.

ASSESSING WORD CREATION

This part of the continuum concerns the process children use to combine letters to make words. At first, children only have knowledge of how words look from having seen words in their environment, and they string letters together to make what looks like a word. The words created in this way are called "mock words" because they are nonphonemic—they do not take into account the sound a letter actually represents (see Figure 7.5a). Children who create mock words have no idea why specific letters make up various words. They determine how many letters (or mock letters) to include based on a logic that is sound to them, but unrelated to how letters are selected in conventional writing. They may decide, for example, that the number of letters they use to write a word should indicate the relative size of the object they are labeling. According to this logic, the word *cat* should be spelled with more letters than the word *kitten* because, of course, a cat is bigger!

(a) Rudimentary letters	"pink"
(b) Closer resemblance to letters	"Sean"
(c) Very close resemblance to letters	"save" sign for block structure

FIGURE 7.4. Examples of actual letters.

When children do begin to attend to how words sound, it is usually at the syllable level, without regard for the individual phonemes that comprise each part of a word. This leads them to create mock words for each syllable they hear as if those syllables are separate words. In this way, they demonstrate early phonological awareness, but not the level of phonemic awareness that would enable them to do alphabetic spelling for word creation. Children who write words that reflect this early level of phonological awareness use any letter in their repertoire to represent the syllable "beats" they hear in a word (see Figure 7.5b). These words are still nonphonemic because letters continue to be used without regard to their assigned sound values.

In time, children do begin to create spellings that are based on an awareness of sound in words at the phoneme level and on the knowledge that letters are used selectively to represent specific sounds in spoken words. Children often use their letter–name knowledge to select letters to represent a sound or two they hear in a word (see Figure 7.5c). Short vowels and other sounds in the middle of words typically are omitted at first. Children usually represent some sounds from the beginning and end of a word. Gradually, children develop more skill in detecting more of the individual sounds they hear in words, and they also know more letter names to use in matching to these sounds (see Figure 7.5d). This level of development is occasionally seen in some preschoolers, but it is not typical in most.

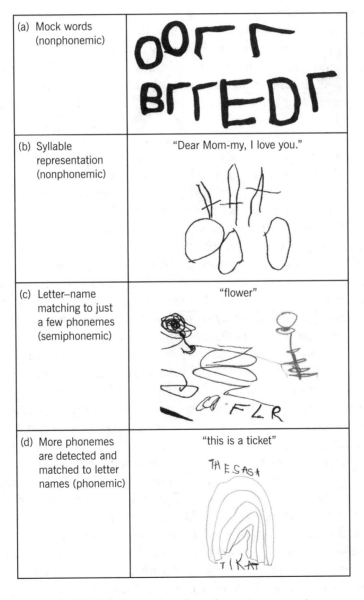

(a)	Mock words (nonphonemic)	
(b)	Syllable representation (nonphonemic)	"Dear Mom-my, I love you."
(c)	Letter–name matching to just a few phonemes (semiphonemic)	"flower"
(d)	More phonemes are detected and matched to letter names (phonemic)	"this is a ticket"

FIGURE 7.5. Examples of word creation strategies.

ASSESSING LEVELS OF MESSAGES

This part of the continuum concerns the content of a child's writing—the meaning a child wants to capture—and the kind of representation used to convey the meaning. One way to judge a message's content level is to consider its length and complexity. A long story is a higher-level message than is a single label for an item a child has drawn; a sentence dictated to describe a drawing is a higher level message than is a single-word label. The appropriateness of a message, of course, depends in part on context. For example, a sign for a play grocery store might have a single label for each food pictured because this is suitable for a sign. If a child is writing a story, however, or describing how caterpillars grew into butterflies, a more detailed message is both possible and suitable. To judge the length and complexity of a child's messages, one considers the context and uses the highest level where it is appropriate to create a long message. To determine program support for message creation, one looks at whether most samples from a class are simple labels or include messages that go beyond these to descriptions of events and to whole stories. It does not matter in judging a message's content level whether the child uses writing-like marks or actual letters, or whether the teacher wrote down the message a child dictated. The focus is the level of the message the child composes, even if the composition is oral as described in Chapter 3.

Figure 7.6 offers a continuum of message creation. It ranges from simple labels (Figure 7.6a) through extended stories (Figure 7.6c). Note that the actual amount of conventional writing does not necessarily vary significantly across some levels, and may in fact be greater in samples of lower message quality. When assessing message creation, it is only the child's intended and stated message that is considered. While there is more actual writing in the child's labeling of the sun in Figure 7.6a than in the get well card in Figure 7.6b, for example, the message itself, "Get better soon," is more elaborated than the simple one-word label for the sun.

A second way to look at the level of written messages is to consider the kind of representational vehicle a child uses. Often, preschoolers use pictures alone to represent their meaning and then support the message with oral explanations. Sometimes, preschoolers combine pictures and writing marks to represent their meaning while continuing to rely on oral language to convey the full meaning, given that neither the graphic system alone or even the two combined can do this. Sometimes preschoolers use only writing marks to convey their meanings, and these can be understood without oral support, as in Figure 7.6d. More often, however, preschoolers' writing marks need the child's oral interpretation because the marks are unconventional. Sometimes, when a child's writing could convey a meaning by itself, it is customary for the artifact created to have illustrations. For all of these reasons, levels of message must be judged with care by considering a variety of samples, collected from a wide variety of social circumstances.

(a) Labels	drawing labeled with child's name 	child's suggestion for new gerbil's name— "Brownie"—taped to cage 	sun 
		B r H m e	*sun*
(b) Phrases or sentences	get well card: "Get better soon" 	page from class book 	page from class book 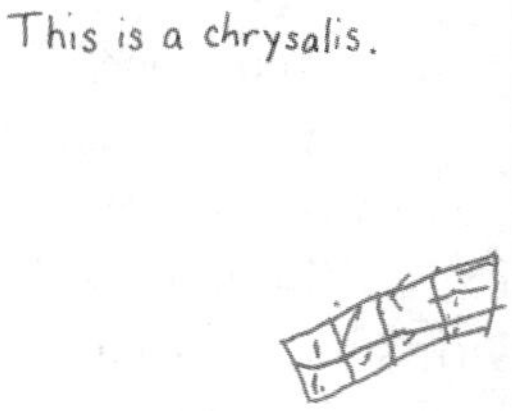
		We opened the cage and let them fly out. *Butterfly*	*This is a chrysalis.*
(c) Stories	page from a long story 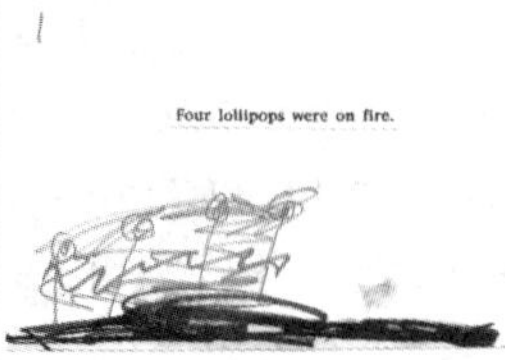	page from a long story 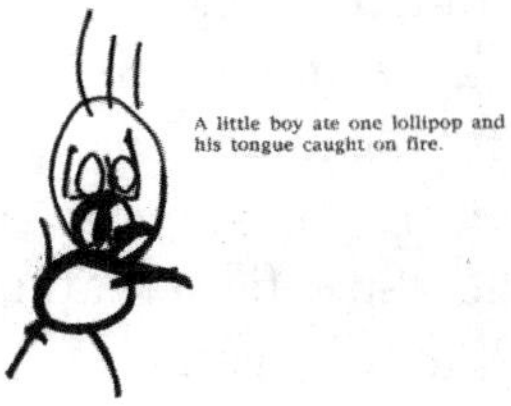	page from a long story 
	Four lollipops were on fire.	A little boy ate one lollipop and his tongue caught on fire.	*The WORM WAS DIGGING A HOLE IN THE EARTH*
(d) Pictureless writing	"phone message" 	"No pets" sign for block play 	"Hi, Grandma. We will be leaving America." 
		NO PATS	*HIGA MAWeWeLBELeR AMArAC*

FIGURE 7.6. Examples of levels of message creation.

INSTRUCTIONAL IMPLICATIONS FROM WRITING ASSESSMENT

Assessment of children's writing is not an exercise done for its own sake. As with all assessment, knowledge of children's understanding of and ability to engage in writing is only meaningful when it used to shape instruction.

Assessment of children's mark making allows us to observe their growing awareness of the alphabet. Teachers can expect to see wide variation in children's mark making during the preschool years. Some children will continue to engage in scribble writing through most of preschool, although we can generally expect most children to notice the linear nature of writing and begin to reflect that in their own writing attempts. Teachers can help children develop this awareness through the shared reading and writing activities described in previous chapters. Making frequent reference to "this line of print" when talking about what is written as part of that routine, while drawing a pointer under the line will help reinforce the linear structure of print.

As children begin to grapple with creating letter-like forms or even writing with some conventional letters, they will benefit from more explicit instruction designed to help them discriminate one letter from another. When children are given explicit instruction about specific letters in accordance with whatever cur-riculum is in place, a writing component should be included. Having children trace letters in sand or shaving cream with their fingers while a teacher demonstrates and verbalizes ("Capital *T*—straight line down, straight line across at the top") will help them not only learn to recognize the different letters, but also to write them. McGee (2007) offers specific verbal instructions for forming each letter of the alphabet. Once these verbal cues are familiar to the children, teachers can use them as needed with individuals who require more assistance as they interact with them in the writing center or during small-group instruction.

Just as their use of marks will vary, so too will preschool children's attempts to create words. All children will benefit from demonstrations of how words are writ-ten. When assessment shows that some children are beginning to produce alpha-betic writing, teachers can work with those children individually to stretch out words and help them listen for more sounds in the words they want to write. Most preschool children are more likely to operate at the syllable level, however, and will not yet be able to do full alphabetic spelling. Helping those children determine how many separate words (or syllables) should be represented will help with their word creation. Such children need to develop the concept of word—that is, that long utterances are actually comprised of smaller chunks called words. Emphasiz-ing the pauses between words while demonstrating writing during shared activities and thinking aloud while writing (e.g., "So far I wrote, 'We are.' The next word is *going*. 'We are going.'") will help children develop the concept of word. A teacher's decision whether to focus on words, syllables, or sounds within syllables should be informed by information from careful assessment that demonstrates children's current level of understanding.

Attention to children's level of message creation should also be informed by assessment. All children will benefit from instruction that makes visible the variety of forms of writing from labels, to lists, to directions, to full stories and sharing of information in expository form. Children who are already capable of telling full stories to accompany their drawing and writing should be praised for their compositions and provided with lots of opportunities for more composing. Children who are less verbal may need individualized interactions with teachers to scaffold creation of longer narratives through questioning that draws out more of their thoughts. Message creation is as much about language development as it is about writing, especially when more of children's meaning is in their verbal explanations of what they have drawn or written than in what actually appears on their papers.

Children who have reached the point in the continuum where they do attempt to write with meaning also need encouragement to extend their written attempts. If they simply label parts of their pictures with single words, a teacher might ask children to elaborate a little more, and then encourage more writing for the extended explanation. For the child who wrote the word *sun* beside the picture in Figure 7.6a, for example, the child might offer the sentence "This sun is bright yellow." The teacher can then provide assistance writing the full sentence, demonstrating for the child the next developmental step in message creation. Again, how the teacher interacts with the child can be driven in part by awareness of the child's current level of understanding and recognition of what is next on the developmental writing continuum.

CONCLUSIONS:
UNDERSTANDING WHAT CHILDREN ARE LEARNING ABOUT WRITING

Preschool teachers must be able to assess children's writing development simultaneously across multiple dimensions. Accurate assessment requires capturing and analyzing examples of children's writing, over time, and from multiple contexts. Teachers must note details of the situations in which writing is produced, including the child's intentions and any support the child received, from written sources in the environment, from peers, or from adults.

For this type of assessment information to be useful, teachers must analyze writing examples for indications of progress in development. Teachers can use the continuum of writing development provided in this chapter to help them recognize significant developmental differences among various pieces of writing. Use of this continuum helps a teacher assess all dimensions of writing skill, which is necessary if a complete and rich picture of a child's writing development is to be obtained.

A Myth about Preschool Writing Assessment

It is too hard to collect and analyze preschool children's writing. They write all the time! I'll only end up with folders crammed with papers for each child. Collecting their drawing and writing just isn't useful.

Preschool children can be prolific with their drawing and writing! But there is no need to keep everything. In fact, children often want to take their creations home at the end of each day. Do keep an assessment folder for each child. But then set up a system for intentionally observing and collecting writing from a small number of children each week. In a typical class of 20 preschool children, focusing on five different children each week will enable you to collect data for each child at least once per month. This allows sufficient time between intentionally collected samples that significant growth will be apparent. It is also the case that once such a system is in place many teachers find they are able to add more focus children each week, decreasing the interval between assessments. Make a point of sitting with those particular children in the writing center and talking with them about what they are doing. Perhaps invite them to create a page for an e-book with you. Watch for any writing they do as they play in centers and capture the resulting artifacts—either placing them in the child's folder with an anecdotal note, or photographing them using your phone to print and add to the child's portfolio later.

Of course, teachers should always be on the lookout for writing samples that demonstrate something interesting about children's development, whether they are the focus of assessment in a particular week or not. Simply being consciously aware of the developmental continua for writing will help you notice when something is significant enough to document. Don't rely on this less systematic observation alone, however, or you may find that you have mountains of artifacts for some children (typically those who frequently clamor for your attention) and much less for others who may be less inclined to include writing in their play or who don't as naturally show you what they have produced.

IDEAS FOR DISCUSSION, REFLECTION, AND ACTION

1. Ask yourself, "How much do I notice what individual children are doing when they write?" Reflect on a typical day in your classroom. Are there particular centers in which children are most likely to write as part of their play? How much time do you spend in those centers so you can observe and document children's writing?

2. How do children use the writing center? Is it used mostly for experimenting with mark making and word creation? Do children use it as a resource for creating books or other extended messages? How might you document children's writing development by observing what they do in the writing center?

3. Work with other preschool teachers and your teaching assistants to set up a schedule for systematically collecting assessment data for the children in your classrooms. Consider specifying a small portion of the time children spend in centers to either shadow particular children or invite them to participate in writing with you while the teaching assistant supervises the remaining children. Carefully consider your daily schedule to find other times

during which you might be able to collect data, including focal children's participation in shared writing, with one of you taking notes (or perhaps video recordings) while the other leads the activity.

4. Consider setting up digital assessment portfolios for the children in your classroom. With other preschool teachers in your school, investigate commercially prepared portfolio systems that might suit your needs and that are compatible with the platforms available (Apple vs. Microsoft computers, iPads vs. other digital tablets, etc.). Or set up your own personalized system. This might be as simple as an e-book *you* create for each child. Add a new page for each assessment activity. Place pictures of the writing artifacts and add your anecdotal notes. These can be supplemented with your own narrative account of what is significant about the particular artifacts, using the audio-recording function of many e-book creation apps. These are ideal to share with parents during parent–teacher conferences and perhaps even e-mail to those who have the technology to open them at home.

References

Amaro-Jiménez, C., & Semingson, P. (2011). Tapping into the funds of knowledge of culturally and linguistically diverse students and families. *NABE News, 33(5)*, 5–9.

Anderson, R. C., Hiebert, E. H., Scott, J. A., & Wilkinson, I. A. G. (1985). *Becoming a nation of readers: The report of the Commission on Reading.* Washington, DC: National Academy of Education, Commission on Education and Public Policy.

Armbruster, B., Lehr F., & Osborn, J. (2003). *A child becomes a reader: Kindergarten through grade 3. Proven ideas from research for parents.* Washington, DC: Partnership for Reading.

Baghban, M. (1984). *Our daughter learns to read and write: A case study from birth to three.* Newark, DE: International Reading Association.

Baroody, A. E., & Dobbs-Oates, J. (2011). Child and parent characteristics, parental expectations, and child behaviours related to preschool children's interest in literacy. *Early Child Development and Care, 181(3)*, 345–359.

Bear, D. R., Invernizzi, M., Templeton, S., & Johnston, F. (2000). *Words their way: Word study for phonics, vocabulary, and spelling instruction* (2nd ed.). Upper Saddle River, NJ: Merrill.

Biemiller, A. (2003). Vocabulary: Needed if more children are to read well. *Reading Psychology, 24*, 323–335.

Biemiller, A. (2006). Vocabulary development and instruction: A prerequisite for school learning. In D. K. Dickinson & S. B. Neuman (Eds.), *Handbook of early literacy research* (Vol. 2, pp. 41–51). New York: Guilford Press.

Burns, M. S., Griffin, P., & Snow C. E. (Eds.). (1999). *Starting out right: A guide to promoting children's reading success.* Washington, DC: National Academy Press.

Burstein, K., & Ergul, C. (2009). *Curriculum based decision making in an early literacy program.* Paper presented at the annual meeting of the American Educational Research Association, San Diego, CA.

Cabell, S., Justice, L., Piasta, S., Curenton, A., Turnbull, K., & Petscher, Y. (2011). The impact of responsivity education on preschoolers' language and literacy skills. *American Journal of Speech–Language Pathology, 20*, 315–330.

Cabell, S., Tortorelli, L., & Gerde, H. (2013). How do I write . . . ?: Scaffolding preschoolers' early writing skills. *The Reading Teacher, 66*(8), 650–659.

Casbergue, R. (2010). Assessment and instruction in early childhood education: Early literacy as a microcosm of shifting perspectives. *Journal of Education. 190*, 13–20.

Casbergue, R., Bedford, A., & Burstein, K. (2014). Class reliability training as professional development for preschool teachers. *Journal of Research in Childhood Education, 28*, 1–14.

Casbergue, R., Burstein, K., & Bedford, A. (2014, December). *Early Reading First Intervention: Children's outcomes after preschool, kindergarten, first, and second grades.* Paper presented at the annual meeting of the Literacy Research Association, Marco Island, FL.

Casbergue, R., McGee, L. M., & Bedford, A. (2008). Characteristics of classroom environments associated with accelerated literacy development. In L. M. Justice & C. Vukelich (Eds.), *Achieving excellence in preschool literacy instruction* (pp. 167–181). New York: Guilford Press.

Cazden, C. B. (1988). *Classroom discourse: The language of teaching and learning.* Portsmouth, NH: Heinemann.

Cherney, I., Seiwert, C., Dickey, T., & Flichtbeil, J. (2006). Children's drawings: A mirror into their minds. *Educational Psychology, 26*(1), 127–142.

Christie, J. (Ed.). (1991). *Play and early literacy development.* Albany: State University of New York Press.

Clay, M. (1975). *What did I write?: Beginning writing behaviour.* Portsmouth, NH: Heinemann.

Clay, M. (1979). *The early detection of reading difficulties: A diagnostic survey with recovery procedures.* Exeter, NH: Heinemann.

Clay, M. (1987). *Writing begins at home: Preparing children for writing before they go to school.* Portsmouth, NH: Heinemann.

Couse, L., & Chen, D. (2010). A tablet computer for young children?: Exploring its viability for early childhood education. *Journal of Research on Technology in Education, 43*(1), 75–98.

Dickinson, D. K., & Porche, M. (2011). Relation between language experiences in preschool classrooms and children's kindergarten and fourth-grade language and reading abilities. *Child Development 82*(3), 870–886.

Fields, M. V. (1998). *Your child learns to read and write.* Olney, MD: Association for Childhood Education International.

Fitzgerald, J., & Amendum, S. (2007). What is sound writing instruction for multilingual learners? In S. Graham, C. A. MacArthur, & J. Fitzgerald (Eds.), *Best practices in writing instruction* (pp. 289–307). New York: Guilford Press.

Ford, K. (2010). Language and literacy development for English language learners in preschool. In M. C. McKenna, S. Walpole, & K. Conradi (Eds.), *Promoting early reading: Research, resources, and best practices* (pp. 37–58). New York: Guilford Press.

Gardner, H. (1980). *Artful scribbles: The significance of children's drawings.* New York: Basic Books.

Gerde, H., Bingham, G., & Wasik, B. (2012). Writing in early childhood classrooms: Guidance for best practices. *Early Childhood Education Journal 40*(6), 351–359.

Gonzalez, N., Moll, L., & Amanti, C. (Eds.). (2005). *Funds of knowledge: Theorizing practices in households, communities, and classrooms.* Mahwah, NJ: Erlbaum.

Goodman, Y. (1981). Test review: Concepts about print test. *The Reading Teacher, 34*(4), 445–448.

Hall, N., & Robinson, A. (2003). *Exploring writing and play in the early years.* London: Fulton.

Hart, B., & Risley, T. (2003). *Meaningful differences in the everyday experience of young American children.* Baltimore: Brookes.

Hresko, W., Herron, S., Peak, P., & Hicks, D. (2012). *Test of early written language* (3rd ed.). New York: Pearson.

International Reading Association & National Association for the Education of Young Children. (1998). *Learning to read and write: Developmentally appropriate practices for young children.* Newark, DE/Washington, DC: Authors.

Invernizzi, M. (2003). Concepts, sounds, and the ABCs: A diet for the very young reader. In D. M. Barone & L. M. Morrow (Eds.), *Literacy and young children: Research-based practices* (pp. 140–156). New York: Guilford Press.

Invernizzi, M., Sullivan, A., Meier, J., & Swank, L. (2004). *Phonological awareness literacy screening.* Charlottesville: University of Virginia Press.

Justice, L. M., Kaderavek, J. N., Fan, X., Sofka, A., & Hunt, A. (20011). Accelerating preschoolers' early literacy development through classroom-based teacher–child storybook reading and explicit print referencing. *Language, Speech and Hearing Services in Schools, 40,* 67–85.

Justice, L. M., Mashburn, A., Hamre, B., & Pianta, R. (2009). Quality of language and literacy instruction in preschool classrooms serving at-risk pupils. *Early Childhood Research Quarterly, 23*(1), 51–68.

Justice, L. M., Mashburn, A., & Petscher, Y. (2013). Very early language skills of fifth-grade poor comprehenders. *Journal of Research in Reading, 36*(2), 172–185.

Kieff, J., & Casbergue, R. (1999). *Playful learning and teaching: Integrating play into preschool and primary programs.* Boston: Allyn & Bacon.

Kieff, J., & Wellhousen, K. (2000). Planning family involvement in early childhood programs. *Young Children, 55*(3), 18–25.

Lankshear, C., & Knobel, M. (2006). *New literacies: Everyday practices and classroom learning* (2nd ed.). New York: Open University Press/McGraw-Hill.

Lankshear, C., & Knobel, M. (2011). *Literacies: Social, cultural, and historical perspectives.* New York: Peter Lang.

Larson, J. (2006). Multiple literacies, curriculum, and instruction in early childhood and elementary school. *Theory into Practice, 45*(4), 319–327.

Larson, L. (2010). Digital readers: The next chapter in e-book reading and response. *The Reading Teacher, 64*(1), 15–22.

Lilly, E., & Green, C. (2004). *Developing partnerships with families through children's literature.* Upper Saddle River, NJ: Merrill/Prentice Hall.

Lisenbee, P. (2009). Whiteboards and web sites: Digital tools for the early childhood curriculum. *Young Children, 64*(6), 92–95.

LoCasale-Crouch, J., Konold, T., Pianta, R., Howes, C., Burchinal, M., Bryant, D., et al. (2007). Observed classroom quality profiles in state-funded pre-kindergarten programs and associations with teacher, program, and classroom characteristics. *Early Childhood Research Quarterly, 22*(1), 3–17.

Lonigan, C., Wagner, R., & Torgesen, J. (2007). *Test of Preschool Early Literacy.* Austin, TX: PRO-ED.

Mashburn, A., Pianta, R., Hamre, B., Downer, J., Barbarin, O., Bryant, D., et al. (2008). Measures of classroom quality in prekindergarten and children's development of academic, language, and social skills. *Child Development, 79*(3), 732–748.

Masonheimer, P. E., Drum, P. A., & Ehri, L. C. (1984). Does environmental print identification lead children into word reading? *Journal of Reading Behavior, 16*(4), 257–271.

McCaslin, N. (1996). *Creative drama in the classroom and beyond* (6th ed.). White Plains, NY: Longman.

McGee, L. (2007). *Transforming literacy practice in preschool.* New York: Scholastic.

McGee, L., & Casbergue, R. (2011). Shifting perspectives in emergent literacy research. In A. McGill-Franzen & R. L. Allington (Ed.), *Handbook of reading disability research* (pp. 185–195). New York: New York: Routledge.

Mendoza, J., & Katz, L. (2008). Introduction to special section on dramatic play. *Early Childhood Research and Practice, 10*(2). Retrieved February 5, 2015, from *http://ecrp.uiuc.edu/v10n2/introduction.html.*

National Association for the Education of Young Children. (2009). *Developmentally appropriate practices in early childhood programs serving children from birth through age eight.* Washington, DC: Author.

National Association for the Education of Young Children & Fred Rogers Center for Early Learning and Children's Media. (2012). Technology and interactive media as tools in early childhood programs serving children from birth through age 8 (Joint position statement). Washington, DC: Authors. Available at *www.naeyc.org/content/technology-and-young-children.*

National Governors Association Center for Best Practices and Council of Chief State School Officers. (2010). *Common Core State Standards for English language arts and literacy, history/social studies, science, and technical subjects.* Washington, DC: Author.

National Early Literacy Panel. (2009). *Developing early literacy: Report of the National Early Literacy Panel.* Washington, DC: National Institute for Literacy.

Northrop, L., & Killeen, E. (2013), A framework for using iPads to build early literacy skills. *The Reading Teacher, 66*(7), 531–537.

Pakarinen, E., Aunola, K., Kiuru, N., Lerkanen, M., Poikkeus, A., Siekkinen, M., et al. (2014). The cross-lagged associations between classroom interactions and children's achievement behaviors. *Contemporary Educational Psychology, 39*(3), 248–261.

Paratore, J. R. (2011). Parents and reading: What teachers should know about ways to support productive home–school environments. In S. J. Samuels & A. E. Farstrup (Eds.), *What research has to say about reading instruction* (4th ed., pp. 406–424). Newark, DE: International Reading Association.

Paratore, J. R., & Edwards, P. A. (2011). Parent–teacher partnerships that make a difference in children's literary achievement. In L. M. Morrow & L. B. Gambrell (Eds.), *Best practices in literacy instruction* (pp. 436–454). New York: Guilford Press.

Pianta, R., LaParo, K., & Hamre, B. (2008). *Classroom assessment scoring system, PK–K.* Baltimore: Brookes.

Piasta, S., & Wagner, R. (2010). *The language and thought of the child.* London: Harcourt & Kegan Paul.

Picard, D., & Gauthier, C. (2012). The development of expressive drawing abilities during childhood and into adolescence. *Child Development Research,* Article ID 925063.

Pilonieta, P., Shue, P., & Kissel, B. (2014). Reading and writing come together in a dual language pre-K classroom. *Young Children, 69*(3), 14–21.

Reutzel, D. R., Fawson, P. C., Young, J. R., Morrison, T. G., & Wilcox, B. (2003). Reading environmental print: What is the role of concepts about print in discriminating young readers' responses? *Reading Psychology, 24*(2), 123–162.

Robins, S., Treiman, R., Rosales, N., & Otake, S. (2012). Parent–child conversations about letters and pictures. *Reading and Writing, 25*(8), 2039–2059.

Roskos, K. A., Ergul, C., Bryan, T., Burstein, K., Christie, J., & Han, M. (2008). Who's learning what words and how fast?: Pre-schoolers' vocabulary growth in an early literacy program. *Journal of Research in Childhood Education, 22*(3), 275–290.

Roskos, K. A., Morrow, L. M., & Gambrell, L. B. (in press). *Oral language and comprehension in preschool: Teaching the essentials.* New York: Guilford Press.

Roskos, K. A., & Neuman, S. B. (1993). Descriptive observations of adults' facilitation of literacy in young children's play. *Early Childhood Research Quarterly, 8*(1), 77–97.

Roskos, K. A., Tabors, P., & Lenhart, L. (2009). *Oral language and early literacy in preschool* (2nd ed.). Newark, DE: International Reading Association.

Rowe, D., & Neitzel, C., (2010). Interest and agency in 2- and 3-year-olds' participation in emergent writing. *Reading Research Quarterly, 45*(2), 169–195.

Rowe, D., & Miller, M. (in press). Designing for diverse classrooms: Using iPads to compose eBooks with emergent bilingual/biliterate four-year-olds. *Journal of Early Childhood Literacy.*

Schickedanz, J. A. (1990). *Adam's righting revolutions: One child's literacy development from infancy through grade one.* Portsmouth, NH: Heinemann.

Schickedanz, J. A. (2003). Engaging preschoolers in code learning: Some thoughts about preschool teachers' concerns. In D. M. Barone & L. M. Morrow (Eds.), *Literacy and young children: Research-based practices. Solving problems in the teaching of literacy* (pp. 121–139). New York: Guilford Press.

Schickedanz, J. A., & Casbergue, R. (2008). *Writing in preschool: Learning to orchestrate meaning and marks.* Newark, DE: International Reading Association.

Schickedanz, J. A., & Dickinson, D., with Charlotte-Mecklenburg Schools. (2005). *Opening the world of learning: A comprehensive early literacy program.* Parsippany, NJ: Pearson Early Learning.

Scull, J. (2013). Assessing language for literacy: A microanalysis of children's vocabulary, syntax and narrative. *International Education Studies, 6*(1), 142–152.

Sénéchal, M., Pagan, S., Lever, R., & Ouellette, G. (2008). Relations among frequency of shared reading and 4-year-old children's vocabulary, morphological and syntax comprehension and narrative skills. *Early Education and Development, 19*(1), 27–44.

Shifflet, R., Toledo, C., & Mattoon, C. (2012). Touch tablet surprises: A preschool teacher's story. *Young Children, 67*(3), 36–41.

Simmerman, S., Harward, S., Pierce, L., Peterson, N., Morrison, T., Korty, B., et al. (2012). Elementary teachers' perceptions of the writing process. *Literacy Research and Instruction, 51*(4), 292–307.

Snow, C. E., Burns, M. S., & Griffin, P. (Eds.). (1998). *Preventing reading difficulties in young children*. Washington, DC: National Academy Press.

Strickland, D. S. (1998). What's basic in beginning reading?: Finding common ground. *Educational Leadership, 55*(6), 6–10.

Strickland, D. S., & Riley-Ayers, S. (2006). Early literacy: Policy and practice in the preschool years. *Preschool Policy Brief, 10*, 1–12.

Sulzby, E. (1985). Children's emergent reading of favorite storybooks: A developmental study. *Reading Research Quarterly, 20*(4), 458–481.

Tabors, P. O. (2008). *One child, two languages: A guide for early childhood educators of children learning English as a second language* (2nd ed.). Baltimore: Brookes.

Treiman, R. (1985). Onsets and rimes as units of spoken syllables: Evidence from children. *Journal of Experimental Child Psychology, 39*(1), 161–181.

Treiman, R., & Broderick, V. (1998). What's in a name?: Children's knowledge about the letters in their own names. *Journal of Experimental Child Psychology, 70*(2), 97–116.

Treiman, R., Cohen, J., Mulqueeny, K., Kessler, B., & Schechtman, S. (2007). Young children's knowledge about printed names. *Child Development, 78*(5), 1458–1471.

U.S. Department of Education. (2015, January). Early Reading First Program. Retrieved from *www2.ed.gov/programs/earlyreading/performance.html*.

Wasik, B., & Hindman, A. (2011). The morning message in early childhood classrooms: Guidelines for best practices. *Early Childhood Education Journal, 39*(3), 183.

Wessels, S., & Trainin, G, (2014). Bringing literacy home: Supporting Latino families' literacy learning. *Young Children, 69*(3), 40–55.

Whitehurst, G., & Lonigan, C. (2010). *Get ready to read, revised*. New York: Pearson.

Wohlwend, K. (2010). A is for avatar: Young children in literacy 2.0 schools and literacy 1.0 schools. *Language Arts, 88*(2), 144–152.

Yelynn. (2012, April 12). Cute little French girl tells a story [Video file]. Retrieved from *www.youtube.com/watch?v=381bv0_Gpo8*.

Yesil-Dagli, U. (2011). Predicting ELL students' beginning first grade English oral reading fluency from initial kindergarten vocabulary, letter naming, and phonological awareness skills. *Early Childhood Research Quarterly, 26*, 15–29.

Yopp, H. K., & Yopp, R. H. (2000). *Oo-pples and boo-noo-noos: Songs and activities for phonemic awareness* (2nd ed.). Orlando, FL: Harcourt.

Children's Literature

Archambault, J., & Martin, B., Jr. (2000). *Chicka chicka boom boom*. New York: Aladdin.

Arnosky, J. (2001). *Rabbits and raindrops*. New York: Puffin.

Lobel, A. (1981). *On Market Street*. New York: Greenwillow.

Ncube, Z. (2012). *Elephant, hippopotamus, and rabbit: The tug of war*. Bloomington, IN: Xlibris.

Numeroff, L. (1985). *If you give a mouse a cookie*. New York: Harper & Row.

Sendak, M. (1979). *Higglety pigglety pop!; or There must be more to life*. New York: Harper & Row.

Williams, S. (1989). *I went walking*. San Diego, CA: Harcourt.

Index

f following and entry indicates a figure; *t* following and entry indicates a table.